Assembly
Poems and Prose

Redvers Brandling

Macmillan Education

First published 1977

Published by
Macmillan Education Limited

Houndmills Basingstoke Hampshire RG21 2XS
and London
Associated companies in New York, Dublin, Melbourne, Johannesburg and Delhi

Printed in England by Cox & Wyman Ltd, Fakenham, Norfolk

Contents

Illustrations

Introduction

One of the main purposes of this book is to provide help with assemblies. That is not to say that the book contains a series of 'packaged assemblies'. I feel that most heads, teachers and groups of children prefer to develop an assembly according to their specific knowledge of the children involved, the local environment and situation, their particular interests, topical events, and many more factors.

There are however features which should be common to all assemblies. As they are times when all, or large numbers, of the school population gather together it is obvious that they are important occasions. They tend to reflect something of the character of the school itself and indeed often possess a quality and ambiance which can be felt better than it can be described.

In consequence they: 'must never be rushed or undignified. Must be serious but not lack humour; never be pompous, pretentious or flippant; should never lack vitality and sincerity'. (B. W. Hearn writing in *Religious Education and the Primary Teacher.*)

They should also, in my opinion, ideally provide opportunities for stimulating thoughts and ideas which can be followed up in the classrooms. In turn this follow-up work can so often inspire fresh lines of thought which can be brought to fruitful culmination by class assemblies.

Thus the whole process of 'assemblies' is really a cycle of events reflecting thoughts, discussions, information, practical activities and concern about wide-ranging issues.

This book offers a selection of poems and prose which, it is hoped, will provide stimulating and thought-provoking material. It was Robert Frost who said that 'poetry begins in delight and ends in wisdom'; and it has been said that 'prose is the literature of knowledge'. Bearing these two statements in mind it will be seen by the reader that all the passages in this book are, to quote a phrase by Rita Snowden, 'made out of life, for life'.

A great many of the selections are without a direct 'moral' as such, but I hope that adults using the book will find much in it to use as, when, and in the context which they think will prove most effective.

In conclusion I would like to offer another thought. Much of the writing in this book is exhilarating. (It is easy to say this when, in the main, to quote Montaigne: 'I have gathered a posie of other men's flowers and nothing but the thread that binds them is my own.') As such it is also suitable for children to read themselves as well as listen to. In consequence the practice of having these selections available in classroom and library can result in most worthwhile suggestions and discussion points arising from the children's comments and opinions. This statement is based, not on assumption, but experience.

Notes on Using the Passages

The linking of the poems and prose passages in this book with a theme is really a question of personal choice. However I have listed a number of themes, and attached to them a selection of passages which seem relevant and stimulating. Thus most of the passages feature in perhaps two or three themes, some are used once only, and in a few instances where they are relevant to a wide variety of issues, some pieces have been used as many as six times.

A head or teacher or class taking assembly based on a theme would therefore have a variety of material from which to choose. Were it to be an isolated assembly they would perhaps choose only one or two passages. If however the theme were to be developed over a number of days then the theme 'recommendations' plus reference to suggested hymns and music could produce a progressive, and linked approach.

Consider, for instance, 'Life'. The selections suggested for this theme include: 'The Thrills and Worries of Hatching', a poem by a junior school girl influenced by the presence of an incubator in her classroom; and 'Saint George's Fair', another observation by a child. 'Lord, I have Time' by Michel Quoist focuses attention on our behaviour during our life span, and 'A Thought' is one of those short encapsulations of great wisdom. 'People Like People' is a plea to break through the narrow confines of our lives and 'Necessities' is a demand that we should do so. 'The Chess Match' is another observation on the importance of tolerance and understanding between age groups.

Thus bracketed together with 'Life' there are poems as short as a few lines and a full length story of eleven hundred words. Authors range from children of average ability to one of the most renowned of religious writers. Thus within this selection there is something for all sections of the primary school.

Should the theme be one for a week then it might form a framework as follows:

Monday: Introductions to theme. Start now! We have time!
Readings: 133 'A Thought'
                selection from 27 'Lord, I have Time'.

Tuesday: Our own lives. How we live them. What we see. What we enjoy.
Readings: 16 'The Thrills and Worries of Hatching'
                20 'St George's Fair'.

Wednesday: Are we too narrow in our outlook? Do we consider too much what other people think about us?
Readings: 183 'People Like People'.

Thursday: Let's consider others. What about people outside our usual group of friends, relatives, etc.?
Reading: 232 'The Chess Match'.

Friday: Conclusions. The need to take stock. Getting our priorities right. Considering our good fortune. Helping others.
Readings: 277 'Necessities?'
                and again
                part of 27 'Lord, I have Time'
                and as the finale
                133 'A Thought'.

The quality of this sort of thematic approach will of course be enhanced by appropriate choices of hymns and music. Two featured hymns for this particular week could therefore be:
'The Family of Man'
'We Shall Overcome'.

Both can be obtained from the same source *Sing Life, Sing Love* published by Holmes MacDougall, and both are suitable for children's instrumental participation.

With regard to recorded music, a look at the details of suggested records at the end of the book will indicate a profusion of material. However if only one record has to be used then it could well be: *Get Together*, BBC RED 147S. This will give opportunity for using such relevant, and attractive, material as 'The Building Song'; 'What is the Meaning of Life?'; 'Morning has Broken'; 'Wonderful World'; and 'Get Together'.

By using the contents of the book in this way it is hoped that five stimulating assemblies could be presented. Hopefully of course this would not be the end of the matter for the work done in the hall should arouse interest, discussion, follow-up work and more ideas from within the classroom. These in turn may be fed back to the school as a whole, thus perpetuating the cycle of interlocking themes, thoughts and presentations which can make assemblies such vital occasions. If this book can help towards achieving the latter then it will have fulfilled its aim.

List of Themes

Poetry

1   Salutation of the Dawn

Look to this day,
for it is the very life of life,
in its brief course lie all the
verities and realities of your existence:
the glory of action,
the bliss of growth,
the splendour of beauty,
for yesterday is but dream and tomorrow is only a vision:
but today well lived makes every yesterday a dream of
   happiness,
and every tomorrow a vision of hope,
Look well, therefore, to this day.

From the Sanskrit

2   Stop the Machines!

The electric mixer is a danger
     to your sanity: it spits the cake mixture
        into your face;
           behind you, the electric kettle
              whistles in complaint.
The hoover runs with a terrible
     sucking, tearing noise
       that rips up the carpet.
The turntable on the record player
     turns the wrong way.
The tea maker gave me a cup of
     water; and the radio clock
       awakened me an hour late:

            the machines are rebelling,
            they wish to rule.
        STOP THEM!   NOW!

Paul Spencer (aged 13)

3   Something Told the Wild Geese

Something told the wild geese
        It was time to go.
Though the fields lay golden
        Something whispered—'Snow'.
Leaves were green and stirring,
        Berries, lustre–glossed,
But beneath warm feathers
        Something cautioned—'Frost'.

All the sagging orchards
        Steamed with amber spice,
But each wild breast stiffened
        At remembered ice.
Something told the wild geese
        It was time to fly—
Summer sun was on their wings,
        Winter in their cry.

Rachel Field

4   Winter's Beauty

Winter is a beautiful time of the year.
But is it?
Frost glistens.
Ice sparkles dazzling white.
This is the beauty of winter.
But the beauty is just a covering,
To a cold miserable world,
Dark and dull,
That starves the animals
Who dare to come out in winter.

Betsy (aged 9)

5 Frankie and Johnny

Frankie and Johnny were lovers.
O Lawdy how they did love!
They swore to be true to each other,
As true as the stars above,
He was her man but he done her wrong.

Frankie went down to the hock shop
Went for a bucket of beer,
Said; 'O Mr Bartender
Has my loving Johnny been here?
He is my man but he's doing me wrong.'

'I don't want to make you no trouble,
I don't want to tell you no lie
But I saw Johnny an hour ago
With a girl named Nelly Bly,
He is your man but he's doing you wrong.'

Frankie went down to the hotel
She didn't go there for fun,
'Cause underneath her kimono
She toted a forty four gun.
He was her man but he done her wrong.

Frankie went down to the hotel.
She rang the front door bell,
Said; 'Stand back all you chippies
Or I'll blow you all to hell.
I want my man for he's doing me wrong.'

Frankie looked in through the keyhole
And there before her eye
Saw her Johnny on the sofa
A-loving up Nelly Bly.
He was her man; he was doing her wrong.

Frankie threw back her kimono,
Took out a big forty four,
Root-a-toot-toot, three times she shot
Right through that hardwood door.
He was her man but he was doing her wrong.

Once more I saw Frankie,
She was sitting in the Electric Chair,
Waiting for to meet her Maker
With the sweat dripping out of her hair.
He was her man but he done her wrong.

This story has no moral,
This story has no end,
This story only goes to show
That there ain't no good in men,
He was her man but he done her wrong.

Anon

6   Gold

Bright, shining, rich,
That's the sign of gold.
People go over mountain, hill and river
Searching for gold.
Searching for it is like looking for
Buttercups in winter.

Kim (aged 8)

7   Change

Change for better,
Or for worse,
At the time, for worse
May be better in the long run.

Deb Smith

8   Freedom

I want to be free
Just like the trees
Like a fragrant summer breeze
Like the radiant moon and sun
And the flowing stars—each one,
        free like the flowers
        free like the birds
        free like hours
        free like words.

I want to be free
Just like the seas
Like a fragrant summer breeze
Like the fields and the hills
Like the tinkling brooks and rills

        free like the flowers *etc*.

I want to be free
Just like the bees
Like a fragrant summer breeze
Like the summer and like spring
Like the birds upon the wing

        free like the flowers *etc*.

Kaye Chudley

9   You

you blue
you red
you yellow
you black
you white
you.

Eugen Gomringer

10 Advice

DO NOT:

        refuse the poor a livelihood,
        tantalise the needy,
        add to the sufferings of the hungry,
        bait a man in distress,
        aggravate a heart already angry,
        keep the destitute waiting for your alms,
        repulse a hard pressed beggar,
        turn your face from a poor man,
        avert your eyes from the destitute,
        give man occasion to curse you,

DO:

        gain the love of the community,
        bow your head to a man of authority,
        listen to the poor man,
        return his greeting courteously,
        save the oppressed from the oppressor,
        be like a father to orphans,
        as good as a husband to widows,
        generous in your gifts to all living,
        share the grief of the grief stricken,
        do not shrink from visiting the sick,
In this way you will make yourself loved.

Adapted from The Jerusalem Bible, *Ecclesiasticus IV*

11 I Wish

I wish I was a butterfly
I could flutter and fly
I would be beautiful
I wish I was a butterfly

Chris (aged 7)

12 Timothy Winters

Timothy Winters comes to school
With eyes as wide as a football-pool,
Ears like bombs and teeth like splinters:
A blitz of a boy is Timothy Winters.

His belly is white, his neck is dark,
And his hair is an exclamation mark.
His clothes are enough to scare a crow
And through his britches the blue winds blow.

When teacher talks he won't hear a word
And he shoots down dead the arithmetic bird,
He licks the pattern off his plate
And he's not even heard of the Welfare State.

Timothy Winters has bloody feet
And he lives in a house on Suez Street,
He sleeps in a sack on the kitchen floor
And they say there aren't boys like him any more.

Old Man Winters likes his beer
And his missus ran off with a bombadier
Grandma sits in the grate with a gin
And Timothy's dosed with an aspirin.

The Welfare Worker lies awake
But the law's as tricky as a six foot snake,
So Timothy Winters drinks his cup
And slowly goes on growing up.

At morning prayers the Headmaster helves *
For children less fortunate than ourselves,
And the loudest response in the room is when
Timothy Winters roars 'Amen!'

*helves: to talk more than is necessary

So come one angel come on ten:
Timothy Winters says 'Amen
Amen amen amen amen.'
Timothy Winters, Lord.

Amen.

Charles Causley

13   We're Going on a Mission

We're going on a mission,
A high adventure mission.
And what will be the end of it is anybody's guess.
We only know our Leader,
We know Him and we trust Him,
And what is good enough for Him is good enough for us.

We're all his special agents,
His highly secret agents;
We may not know each other and we may not often speak.
But weekly at Headquarters
We're all of us together,
We're there to get our briefing and our rations for the week.

It helps you with your courage
To know that you're with others,
But often you're on solo and it isn't very nice.
But that is why our Leader
Has given us permission
To call him on the inter-com and ask for his advice.

We're going on a mission,
A most important mission,
And what will be the end of it is anybody's guess.
We only know our Leader
Has done it all before us,
And what is good enough for Him is good enough for us.

Michael Hewlett

14 Hypocrite

She spoke of heaven
And an angelic host;
She spoke of God
And the Holy Ghost;
She spoke of Christ's teachings
Of man's brotherhood;
Yet when she had to sit beside a Negro once—
She stood.

Elizabeth Hart

15 Hedgehog

The snail moves
Like a hovercraft,
Held up by a rubber
Cushion of itself, sharing the secret

With the hedgehog. The hedgehog
Shares its secret with no one.
We say, 'Hedgehog, come out
Of yourself and we will love you.

We mean no harm. We want
Only to listen to what
You have to say. We want
Your answers to our questions.'

The hedgehog gives nothing
Away, keeping itself to itself.
We wonder what a hedgehog
Has to hide, why it so distrusts.

We forget the God
Under His crown of thorns.
We forget that never again
Will a God trust in the world.

Paul Muldoon

16 The Thrills and Worries of Hatching

It's still and silent in the world of chicks,
But nature's still at work,
No matter where it might lurk.
The eggs are still and silent,
The world has not begun,
For the chicks the embryo that lays inside
Is a silent unmoving oval shaped ball.
Then it all begins!
An egg has been pierced,
A little beak comes through.
The chicks will think we're giants,
They'll think that about you.

Written by a child when there was an incubator in her classroom

17 Love?

If I were loved
        I'd be content,
Even hate
        I'd understand,
But please
        Don't tolerate me
That's something
        I can't stand.

The tolerators
        Nod their heads
And smile
        Their tolerant smile,
But please
        Try to love or hate
Me for
        A little while.

Alan Martin

18 Old Age

An old lady walks down the street,
A stick in each hand.
She walks slowly, hunched up.
She looks forlorn and helpless.
She asks somebody to help her across the road.
They look at her shabby coat
And then they turn away.
The old lady tries to cross the road but she can't.
She needs glasses but she can't afford them. She's poor.
Her face wrinkles as she goes back into her house.

Maureen (aged 10)

19 Bottles and People

See that bottle over there
I don't want to be like it.
I can touch it and feel it
But when I tip it up
It's empty.
There's nothing in it—just air.
People have shapes
A bit like bottles.
There's bulges and bottoms and mouths.
But it's what's inside them that counts.
If they're kind and cheerful
And friendly and good to be with
And helpful and thoughtful
These things seem to come out
And never stop.
If they're mean and nasty
Don't care about you
But only themselves
They seem like empty bottles
Full of nothing but air.

Elizabeth (aged 10)

20   Saint George's Fair

Shouting, screaming, whistling, cheering,
I wonder what I can hear?
It sounds like something's going on.
I must go and see.
Could be a fight, could be anything.
I'll have to go and see.
I can see people, flags, stalls.
It must be a fair.
I must go and see what it is like.
Hey! There's Mr Groves and Mr Snow.
I wonder what they are doing here.
There is a bear. He looks nice.
Hey! There's a man on stilts!
There's a man on someone's hands, upside down. That's clever!
There are lots of stalls.
Oh! I have just got time for a chicken, because they are closing
   down.
I wish I could have come earlier, but I was somewhere else.
I will be earlier next year.

Jan (aged 8)

21   Is Today Your Birthday?

If today is your birthday
It is a favourable one.
Don't expect sudden riches
Or unexpected surprises.
Your success will be quiet.
You will be rewarded for your hard work.
If you are employed you may get promotion.
If you are an employer you can expect good prospects.
Love affairs will run smoothly,
Your lucky number could be six
And watch out for the colour blue.

From a newspaper horoscope of the 1930s

22   The Victim Died of Stab Wounds

It was when the novelty of life
Wore off he bought a flick.knife;
And the leather jacket he stole
Because it was a status symbol
That helped him to play it cool,
To prove he was nobody's fool.

Then he ganged up. He was only
Doing what insecure, lonely
Types do, as the psychiatrist
Pointed out. Put to the test,
He had no option but to climb
The ladder of petty crime.

What's more vulnerable than age?
A man counting dough in his dotage,
Before the shop door shuts,
Asks for it. But it takes guts
To grab the loot and scarper
Under the busy nose of a copper.

You don't expect old men to show
Fight, to bellow, to blow
A referee's whistle. It's a life
For a life. The flick knife
Burns in the sweating palm
Of the hand that means no harm.

It's that simple. As for death,
What is it? You buy a wreath,
Pull down a blind, drink a pint
In memory of some old skinflint,
Then put it out of your mind
Until you next pull down a blind.

A death is natural. A killing
Is a special sort of thing.
The slob had let him down by dying;
He lay there not even trying
To live. The flick knife stuck
Out of him. What bloody luck!

It's the enormity of the offence
Proves, in a way, its innocence.
Not that this helped him much
Before the Bench. He lost touch
Somehow with himself. Disgrace
Stamped on a magistrate's face

Didn't register. What maybe did
Was the shock of the blood
Trickling slowly into a crack.
If he could, he would have put it back
Into the body. That he never can
Makes him, prematurely, a man.

F. Pratt Green

23   The Dance of Life

Like a wild highland fling my youth began,
With many a stamp and shout.
I danced through my teens with a light quick step,
So happy, and carefree and unrestricted,
I launched into the foxtrot of marriage.

Slowly I came to adult maturity,
Matured like a piece of cheddar,
With a stately waltz, my forties I reached,
With slow precision, and steady steps.
Now sure of myself I end my life,
Dancing my dance of a minuet,
Rejoicing in the dance of life.

Kim Ford (aged 15)

24 The New Boy

The door swung inward. I stood and breathed
The new school atmosphere:
The smell of polish and disinfectant,
And the flavour of my own fear.

I followed into the cloakroom; the walls
Rang to the shattering noise
Of boys who barged and boys who banged;
Boys and still more boys!

A boot flew by me. Its angry owner
Pursued with force and yell;
Somewhere a man snapped orders; somewhere
There clanged a warning bell.

And there I hung with my new schoolmates;
They pushing and shoving me; I
Unknown, unwanted pinned to the wall;
On the verge of ready-to-cry.

Then, from the doorway, a boy called out:
'Hey, you over there! You're new!
Don't just stand there propping the wall up!
I'll look after you!'

I turned; I timidly raised my eyes;
He stood and grinned meanwhile;
And my fear died, and my lips answered
Smile for his smile.

He showed me the basins, the rows of pegs;
He hung my cap at the end;
He led me away to my new classroom . . .
And now that boy's my friend.

John Walsh

25 Boy

Mum'll be coming home today.
It's three weeks she's been away.
When Dad's alone all we eat
is cold meat
which I don't like
and he burns the toast I want just-brown
and I hate taking the ash-can down.

He's mended the door
from the little fight
on Thursday night
so it doesn't show
and we can have grilled tomatoes
Spanish onions and roast potatoes
and will you sing me 'I'll never more roam'
when I'm in bed, when you've come home.

Michael Rosen

26 Life

Birth is like a car just come off a production line,
Clean, glittering and ready to go.

Childhood is like a car keen to do well
And always trying its best.

Youth is like a car large and bossy and tough,
Always knocking younger cars around.

Maturity is like a car that is sensible
And knows that in a crisis it has to do fifty miles per gallon.

Old age is like a car that is rusty,
Squeaky, slow and unwanted.

Death is like a car turfed onto a scrapheap
And melted down into nothing.

Stuart Porteous

27 Lord, I Have Time

I went out, Lord.
Men were coming out.
They were coming and going,
Walking and running.
Everything was rushing, cars, lorries, the street, the whole
    town.
Men were rushing not to waste time.
They were rushing after time.
To catch up with time,
To gain time.

Goodbye Sir, excuse me, I haven't time.
I'll come back, I can't wait, I haven't time.
I must end this letter—I haven't time.
I'd love to help you, but I haven't time.
I can't accept, having no time.
I can't think, I can't read, I'm swamped, I haven't time.
I'd like to pray, but I haven't time.

You understand, Lord, they simply haven't the time.
The child is playing, he hasn't time right now . . . Later on . . .
The schoolboy has his homework to do, he hasn't time . . .
        Later on . . .
The student has his courses, and so much work, he hasn't
    time . . .
        Later on . . .
The young man at his sports, he hasn't time . . . Later on . . .
The young married man has his new house, he has to fix it up,
    he hasn't time . . . Later on . . .
The grandparents have their grandchildren, they haven't
    time . . .
        Later on . . .
They are dying, they have no . . .
Too late! . . . They have no more time!

And so all men run after time, Lord.
They pass through life running-hurried, jostled, overburdened,
    frantic, and they never get there. They haven't time.

In spite of all their efforts they're still short of time,
  of a great deal of time.
Lord you must have made a mistake in your calculations.
There is a big mistake somewhere.
The hours are too short,
The days are too short,
Our lives are too short.

You who are beyond time, Lord, you smile to see us fighting it.
And you know what you are doing.
You make no mistakes in your distribution of time to men.
You give each one time to do what you want him to do.

But we must not lose time
    waste time,
     kill time,
For time is a gift that you gave us,
But a perishable gift,
A gift that does not keep.

Lord, I have time,
I have plenty of time,
All the time that you give me.

The years of my life,
The days of my years,
The hours of my days,
They are all mine.
Mine to fill, quietly, calmly,
But to fill completely, up to the brim,
To offer them to you, that of their insipid water
You may make a rich wine such as you once made in Cana of
  Galilee.

I am not asking you tonight, Lord, for time to do this and then
    that,
But your grace to do conscientiously, in the time that you give
  me,
    what you want me to do.

Michel Quoist

28 Carol

The Palm Court Lounge is snug and warm
There's Scotch on every table
It's not our fault it's not so hot
Next door in the hotel stable.

The passengers are drunk tonight
The crew have cash to burn
So who will hear the drowning man
We've left ten miles astern?

Let's all go down the Motorway
And see who's first at Chester
Let's forget that scruffy dog
We knocked for six at Leicester.

O we're all right and so is Jack
(He's underneath the table)
It's not our fault it's not so hot
Next door in the hotel stable.

God rest us merry, Gentlemen,
This is no time for sorrow
Because ten thousand refugees
Will get no grub tomorrow.

The Landlord smiles and lays the bill
Quite gently on the table
The man who'll pay has just been born
Next door in an ice-cold stable.

Ronald Deadman

29 Youth

Youth is a splendid time.
I think everybody ought to be young once.

Daniel George

30 'General, that Tank'

General, that tank of yours is some car.
It can wreck a forest, crush a hundred men.
But it has one failing:
It needs a driver.

General, you've got a good bomber there.
It can fly faster than the wind, carry more than an elephant
    can.
But it has one failing:
It needs a mechanic.

General, a man is a useful creature.
He can fly, and he can kill.
But he has one failing:
He can think.

Bertolt Brecht

31 Nativity

I can't hear the angels—
The bombs roar and slay:
            Somewhere a baby
            Is wounded and crying,
            And somewhere a baby is crying.

I don't need to look for
A stable today:
            Somewhere the homeless
            Are searching and trying,
            And somewhere a baby is crying.

I can't see the manger—
The feast's in the way:
            Somewhere the people
            Are hungry and dying,
            And somewhere a baby is crying.

Cecily Taylor

32 Treasure?

. . . So don't store up your treasure on earth
Where it grows rusty and moth eaten
And thieves break in to steal it.
So store up your treasure in heaven
Where there is no rust and no moths
And no thieves break in to steal it.
For where your treasure is
So will your heart be also . . .

From the song 'All Good Gifts' from Godspell, *music and lyrics by Stephen Schwartz*

33 I Don't Understand

(On viewing a courting couple sitting on some church steps!)

Soppy things,
They'll catch a chill
On the steps.
It's silly really.
Why?
Because, well, because
I don't understand,
And what I don't understand
I don't like.
Well if I was going to do . . .
Well, that,
I wouldn't do it there,
On the steps,
Catching a chill.
Or perhaps they're not
Catching a chill.
Perhaps it's warm.
Perhaps, perhaps . . .
I don't understand.

Sara Reid (aged 12)

34 Forever

Forever is a word to beware,
Forever is for always,
Never ending
But everything must end,
So forever is never forever
Only for now,
Till now ends.

Deb Smith

35 Working for People

There is no point in work
Unless it's for people,
For definite people.

If it isn't for people,
For definite people.
Don't do it.

Then every work is a life work,
And to work is to live freely, joyously and abundantly,
And in such living the spirit sings,
And people come before things.

So when a man is peeling potatoes,
And under his hands the mud and the dirt and the skin are cut
            away,
Even the last eye and speck will be cut out
When he thinks, 'This is for a friend to eat,
And he may never know my care,
But he will feel it, and be glad.'

John Morrison

36 I Tried

I tried to do some knitting,
I tried and tried and tried.
But all the holes and knots and things,
I just couldn't hide.

I tried to do some painting,
An Indian, colours bright.
Then my paint brush slipped, it smudged my work
So that it didn't turn out right.

I tried to do some sewing,
An apron or perhaps a scarf.
The scissors slipped,
And then I found, I'd cut my work in half.

So now I've turned to cooking,
I hope I will succeed.
Eggs, sugar, milk and flour,
These are things I'll need.

Well, I tried.

Diane Lewis (aged 11)

37 War

She was sitting on the rough embankment,
her cape too big for her tied on slapdash
over an odd little hat with a bobble on it,
her eyes brimming with tears of hopelessness.
An occasional butterfly floated down
fluttering warm wings onto the rails.
The clinkers underfoot were deep lilac.
We got cut off from our grandmothers
while the Germans were dive-bombing the train.
Katya was her name. She was nine.

From 'The Companion' by Yevgeny Yevtushenko

38 Life's Just a Puzzle

To me each day is a giant jigsaw waiting to be assembled.
Bits of sky and broken clouds,
Bright red buses, bustling crowds,
Different emotions, edges of fun,
Corners of buildings, rays of sun,
Fitting the minutes, linking the hours
With tears and rainbows, laughter and flowers.

Sylvia Mariconda (aged 13)

39 My Mother Saw a Dancing Bear

My mother saw a dancing bear
By the schoolyard, a day in June.
The keeper stood with chain and bar
And whistle-pipe, and played a tune.

And bruin lifted up its head
And lifted up its dusty feet,
And all the children laughed to see
It caper in the summer heat.

They watched as for the Queen it died.
They watched it march. They watched it halt.
They heard the keeper as he cried,
'Now, roly-poly!' 'Somersault!'

And then, my mother said, there came
The keeper with a begging-cup,
The bear with burning coat of fur,
Shaming the laughter to a stop.

They paid a penny for the dance,
But what they saw was not the show;
Only, in bruin's aching eyes,
Far distant forests, and the snow.

Charles Causley

40   Foggy Day

The street lamps and the lights
        Upon the halted cars
Could either be on earth
        Or be the heavenly stars.

A man passed by me close.
        I asked the way. He said
'Come follow me, my friend.'
        I followed where he led.

He tapped the stones in front.
        'Trust me, my friend, and come.'
I followed like a child.
        A blind man led me home.

Patricia French (aged 11)

41   The Car

We had been driving along the road for hours.
The country, towns and villages whizzed by.
The car is a fast thing.
If somebody from the past were to come into our world
He would think it was a monster;
A growling, zooming monster,
A thing not from this earth.
Cars let off fumes.
Cars are fast.
Cars make dirt.
In many ways a car is a miraculous thing.
It is something that nature did not build.
But it is a monster.
It does growl.
It roars like a monster.
It looks like a monster.
But . . . that is a car!

Susan (aged 10)

42   Diamond Cobwebs

Like diamond necklaces
Are cobwebs covered in dew,
Nature's wheels all glistening
In the bushes,
Or trampolines and nets
Just ready for the springing,
Or dragons' caves among the grass
Which are luminous after dark,
And ferris wheels that never go around.
The webs in the morning
Are like jewelled palaces
Scintillating in the sun.

Adrian Cherry (aged 10)

43   Release

They gave me ten years
I'm free today.
I want to run around
And shout 'Hurray'.

I make new friends
But they all give me the shove
When they learn I've been inside
And deserve no love.

I do my utmost
To make amends
But it makes no difference
The hate never ends.

I wonder what they'll do?
Will they take back all they said?
When they find the gas on
And me lying dead.

James (aged 13)

44   The Puddle

Here are the moon
And a passing bird
Held in a puddle;
Isn't life a muddle?
Isn't it absurd
To think that very soon
All the city folk
Hastening to and fro,
Will splash and never know
Though their ankles soak,
That this clouded thing
Held a moon and a wing?

Celia Randall

45   The Donkey

When fishes flew and forests walked
And figs grew upon thorn,
Some moment when the moon was blood
Then surely I was born;

With monstrous head and sickening cry
And ears like errant wings,
The devil's walking parody
On all four footed things.

The tattered outlaw of the earth,
Of ancient crooked will;
Starve, scourge, deride me; I am dumb,
I keep my secret still.

Fools! For I also had my hour;
One far fierce hour and sweet:
There was a shout about my ears,
And palms before my feet.

G. K. Chesterton

46 Tree of Life

Birth is like a tree,
Springing out of the ground,
Green and fresh.

Then comes childhood,
Growing branches and leaves,
Playing in the wind as it sways about.

Youth is next,
As the tree grows stout and strong,
Standing up against the wind.

Then maturity,
And the seeds drop from the branches,
And start a new generation.

Then ripe old age,
And your nearing death
As your withered branches start to drop.

Then last of all, death,
As the storm blows up
And the lightning strikes. Death.

Nicholas Farraway

47 The Spider or the Web?

Ugh what a horrible thing
Round, hairy, solid and black.
Scrawling, creeping, dandy legged.
But the web . . .
Shining like silver in the sun
Glittering in the morning dew
A twinkling pattern of delicate lace.
How can something so ugly
Make something so fragrant and fresh?

Alison (aged 11)

48   The Wreckers' Prayer

Give a wrack or two, Good Lard,
For winter in Tops'il Tickle be hard.
Wid grey frost creepin' like mortal sin
And perishin' lack of bread in the bin.

A grand rich wrack, us do humbly pray,
Busted abroad at the break o'day
An' hove clear in 'crost Tops'il Reef,
Wid victuals an' gear to beguile our grief.

God of reefs an' tides an' sky,
Heed ye our need and hark to our cry!
Bread by the bag an' beef by the cask—
Ease for sore bellies bes all we ask.

One grand wrack—or maybe two?—
Wid gear an' victuals to see us through
'Til spring starts up like the leap of day
An' the fish strike back into Tops'il Bay.

One rich wrack—for They hand bes strong!
A barque or a brig from up-along
Bemused by they twisty tides, O Lard!
For winter in Tops'il Tickle bes hard.

Loud an' long will us sing yer praise.
Merciful Fadder, O Ancient of Days,
Master of fog, an' tide, an' reef!
Heave us a wrack to beguile our grief.

                                                    Amen.

Theodore Goodridge Roberts

49 Milk Man

The milk man is a nice man
Who brings us milk each day.
I like to bring the milk in
But my mum says it's naughty in some way.

Barrie (aged 8)
This poem was quoted in an article on environmental studies

50 Definition

What is war my lord?
War is empire.

What is war general?
War is manhood.

What is war teacher?
War is inevitable.

What is war preacher?
War is unfortunate.

What is war fellow?
War is escape.

What is war kind employer?
War is profit.

Sister what is war?
War is a telegram.

Brother what is war?
War is my impotency.

Father what is war?
War is my trembling hands.

Mother what is war?
War is three undiscovered graves.

Laurence Collinson

51   Recipe

Double, double here comes trouble,
The leg of a lion
An old piece of iron.
The tail of a cat
The head of a rat.
Some blood from a dog
The wood of a log.
Bubble, bubble there goes trouble.

Schoolboy (aged 7)

52   New Year Carol

Here we bring new water
              from the well so clear,
For to worship God with,
              this happy New Year.

Sing levy dew, sing levy dew,
              the water and the wine;
The seven bright gold wires
              and the bugles that do shine.

Sing reign of Fair Maid,
              with gold upon her toe,
Open you the West Door,
              and turn the Old Year go.

Sing reign of Fair Maid
              with gold upon her chin,
Open you the East Door,
              and let the New Year in.

Sing levy dew, sing levy dew,
              the water and the wine;
The seven bright gold wires
              and the bugles they do shine.

Traditional

53   The Salesman

There's plenty of words
And a ready smile.
A cigarette exchanged
And a confidence dropped.
Money? A shrug and a sigh.
How sad that it need
Even be mentioned.
But now that it is,
Movements seem brisker.
The eye seems to harden
And set on some goal.
There's talk of inflation
And discount and terms.
A Biro and papers,
White cuffs and gold links,
All shuffle round in a whirl.
Let's clinch it Old Boy,
It's a deal!
The smile's readjusted,
Good manners return.
How's the wife?
You'll enjoy it.
That's your copy there.
He's gone and you're left
With a purpled tissue.
A trivial thing and yet enough
To buy time and attention
In a world of
Words without meaning
And smiles without feeling.

Stan Hodgson

54   Brrrr Brrrr

The telephone stands in the hall,
White, shiny, silent.
I watch it.
I want it to shatter the silence with its loud brrrr brrrr.
I want to be first to pick up the smooth receiver,
To say Hello and give our number.
But most of all I want the call to be for me.

Elizabeth (aged 8)

55   Man's Pilgrimage

First, birth:
The beginning:
The start of the way.

Then infancy:
An easy time,
Without a burden on your back.

Then childhood:
A happy road of flowers,
When all is gay and careless.

Then youth:
When you hope and dream
and love.

Then maturity:
When cares set in,
And you can lose your joy of God
For love of earthly things.

Then age:
The end of earthly bondage.
And the sound of trumpets you discern
And the wanderer's return.

M. J. Welsh (aged 12)

56　Appearances

The poor man's wisdom keeps his head erect,
　　　and gives him a place with the great.

Do not praise a man for his good looks,
　　　nor dislike anybody for his appearance.

Small among winged creatures is the bee
　　　but her produce is the sweetest of the sweet.

Ecclesiasticus XI 1–3

57 Fox

Exploiter of the shadows
He moved among the fences,
A strip of action coiling
Around his farmyard fancies.

With shouting fields are shaken,
The spinneys give no shelter;
There is delight for riders,
For hounds a tooth in shoulder.

The creature tense with wildness
Knows death is sudden falling
From fury into weary
Surrendering of feeling.

Clifford Dyment

58 Hope

Tired nerves twitchin from sorrow and care
Tired feet itchin to take me somewhere
Southland bewitchin, beckons me there.
Hard times, that's all we hear round this way
Odd times they're growin thinner each day.
Good times
'Just 'round the corner,' so they say.

From 'Way Down South Where the Blues Began' by W. C. Handy

59 Joseph Came to Somers Town

Stay! Stay! good travellers all, for God is born a Man
And lies wrapped in a table cloth within a railway van.

Joseph came to Somers Town, behind the Euston Road,
Evicted from his caravan and now of no abode;
Mary sought a lodging there, shelter for her head,
But all the jostling houses could offer them no bed.
Stay! O Stay! good travellers all, for God is born a Man
And lies wrapped in a table cloth within a railway van.

So Mary came to Euston, where a porter found them room
In a shunted unused guard's van half shrouded in the gloom.
And there with no possessions, no midwife standing by,
There rang throughout the station, her new born baby's cry.
Stay! O Stay! good travellers all, for God is born a Man
And lies wrapped in a table cloth within a railway van.

The porters came and wished her luck and brought them cups
            of tea,
And as the rumour spread around there came to Platform Three
The other weary travellers, who travelled Christmas Day,
And offered Him a tribute, then turned and went their way.
Stay! O Stay! good travellers all, for God is born a Man
And lies wrapped in a table cloth within a railway van.

Douglas Brice

60   Taking the Hands

Taking the hands of someone you love,
You see they are delicate cages . . .
Tiny birds are singing
In the secluded prairies
And in the deep valleys of the hand.

Robert Bly

61   Cena

A crowded Last
Supper, thirteen heads,
Twenty-six hands, some
Under the table's
Long linenfold skirts,
Elbows getting in the way,
Feet in sandals kicked
Under the stout trestles,
Fingers dipped in dishes,
Breaking bread, carafe
Decanting acid wine,
Dark, muddy, poor stuff,
John, James, Judas,
Even the betrayer
His face tanned by a golden halo
Turned all in profile
And the thirteen auras
All at different heights
Bob and jostle above
The tablecloth's white Jordan
Like balloons, buoys, mooring lights.

In mid-channel
One full face
In solitude.

James Kirkup

62 The Garden Shed

There is one particular corner in our garden shed:
Upon the polythene bags of compost lie three cracked flower
        pots.
Next to these a burst bag of sand lies, shrouding the bowl
        of golden brown ground bait.
The fishing rods, up against the wall, dusty from the close
        seasonal disuse.
Above these, three rusty nails, crudely slapped in, support the
        grit covered shovel.
This is the corner where so many times I have retired to sit
        down
and think in the half light that sieves through the dusty
        windows.
This is the corner of my life.

Mark Keath (aged 13)

63 Christmas

Christmas is:

        a jolly time,
        for seeing holly,
        for throwing snowballs,
        for getting presents.

Christmas is:

        a happy time,
        for families together,
        for giving and getting,
        for thinking of Jesus.

Christmas is:

        enjoying,
        sharing,
        remembering,
        living.

Jimmy (aged 10)

64   Happiness

Do not abandon yourself to sorrow,
           do not torment yourself with brooding.
Gladness of heart is life to a man,
           joy is what gives him length of days.
Beguile your cares, console your heart,
           chase sorrows far away;
For sorrow has been the ruin of many,
           and is no use to anybody.
Jealousy and anger shorten your days,
           and worry brings premature old age.
A genial heart makes a good trencherman,
           one who benefits from his food.

Ecclesiasticus XXX 21–27

65   Just Like a Man

He sat at the dinner table
With a discontented frown,
The potatoes and steak were underdone
And the bread was baked too brown;
The pie was too sour and the pudding too sweet,
And the roast was much too fat;
The soup so greasy, too, and salt,
'Twas hardly fit for the cat.

'I wish you could eat the bread and pie
I've seen my mother make,
They are something like, and 'twould do you good
Just to look at a loaf of her cake.'
Said the smiling wife, 'I'll improve with age—
Just now I'm but a beginner;
But your mother has come to visit us,
And to-day she cooked the dinner.'

Anon

66 Generosity

Nevertheless, be patient with those who are badly-off,
> do not keep them waiting on your generosity.
For the commandment's sake go to the poor man's help,
> do not turn him away empty-handed in his need.
Better let your silver go on brother or friend,
> Do not let it go to waste, rusting under a stone.

Ecclesiasticus XXIX 8–13

67 The Man Who Finds That His Son Has Become a Thief

Coming into the store at first angry
At the accusation, believing in
The word of his boy who has told him:
I didn't steal anything, honest.

Then becoming calmer, seeing that anger
Will not help in the business, listening painfully
As the other's evidence unfolds, so painfully slow.

Then seeing gradually that evidence
Almost as it tightens slowly around the neck
Of his son, at first vaguely circumstantial,
> then gathering damage,
Until there is present the unmistakable odour of guilt
Which seeps now into the mind and lays its poison.

Suddenly feeling sick and alone and afraid,
As if an unseen hand had slapped him in the face
For no reason whatsoever: wanting to get out
Into the street, the night, the darkness, anywhere to hide
The pain that must show in the face to these strangers, the fear.

It must be like this.
It could hardly be otherwise.

Raymond Souster

68 The Old Grey Goose

Go and tell Aunt Nancy,
Go and tell Aunt Nancy,
Go and tell Aunt Nancy,
   The old grey goose is dead.

The one that she was saving,
The one that she was saving,
The one that she was saving,
   To make a feather bed.

I saw her a-dying,
I saw her a-dying,
I saw her a-dying,
   With her wing tucked over her head.

She died on Friday,
She died on Friday,
She died on Friday,
   Behind the old barn shed.

She left nine little goslings,
She left nine little goslings,
She left nine little goslings,
   To scratch for their own bread.

Anon

69 Daffodils

When I look at a daffodil with its big trumpet,
   I listen to it.
It sounds like the sea.
   I shut my eyes to listen to it.
It sings a song whispering to me
   beneath its trumpet.
I don't know what it says to me.
   Daffodils, daffodils, swaying in the wind.

Andrew Stork (aged 7)

70 Kindness

A loving arm
Shelters me
From any harm.

The shelteredness
Of kindness
Flows around me.

Mary Flett (aged 9)

71 Limerick

There was a young lady called Perkins,
Who was very fond of small gherkins;
One day at tea,
She ate forty three
And pickled her entire workings!

Cindy Spurr (aged 11)

72 The Sea Under the Moon

The sea was a gigantic basin of milk,
Still and silent.
The moon sent down soft golden rays
Shining like a million fireflies.
They fingered the sea,
Inquisitively gliding over the murmuring ripples,
Making the sea shine
As though pieces of gold were glinting
Under the water.
Then a warning of light shone over the horizon,
And the glory of night
Disappeared for another twelve hours,
In the other world.

Susan (aged 11)

73   The Hero of the Match

When the Rovers played United in the final yesterday
The factories stopped working and declared a holiday.
On foot, in cars and buses, folk came from miles around
To see the two unbeaten teams meet on the valley ground.

The winter sun was shining and a chill was in the air;
A bitter wind was blowing but no one seemed to care.
They sang and laughed and whistled, and oh but it was grand
To hear the mighty cheer they gave as the players left the
    stand.

United were the bigger team, they played in black and white;
They were fearsome in the tackle and they dearly loved a fight.
Their defence was firm and steady, their attack knew how to
    shoot,
And their centre-forward, Banger, was a nasty vicious brute.

The Rovers were a smaller lot, they played in gold and blue;
Their movements were delightful, their passes straight and
    true.
They could trap and shoot and dribble and they really knew
    the game.
Their captain was the goalkeeper—Bill Sprightly was his name.

The referee blew his whistle and the tussle had begun.
United's burly winger made a fast and dangerous run,
But the Rovers' full-back tackled him as quickly as he could
And kicked the ball out swiftly to where his forwards stood.

Then back and forth the struggle raged and neither side could
    gain
For United had the strength and force but Rovers had the brain
At every shot and corner the clubs' supporters roared,
But when the half time whistle went—neither side had scored!

When the second half had started the Rovers had the ball;
Jim the half-back took it and passed it on to Paul.
He beat United's full-back, swerved, and gave a shout
As he kicked it past the goalie, who was slow in coming out.

A goal! The crowd was roaring and United gave a groan
But Banger set his teeth and swore he'd win the match alone.
When the centre had been taken he started the attack
And charged a Rovers' forward in the middle of the back.

For half an hour United fired shots into the goal
But Sprightly was unbeatable—he saved them one and all.
Then Banger rushed in madly. He charged with all his might,
And when they picked Bill Sprightly up his face was very
    white.

His left arm hung down limply, his face was streaked with
    blood;
His hands and knees were painful where he'd fallen in the
    mud.
But he pushed the helpers from him and stood, all stiff and
    sore,
In the goal-mouth, undefeated, to keep them out once more.

Five minutes to the whistle! The minutes seemed like hours!
Five minutes to the whistle and then the cup is ours!
So the Rovers hung on grimly, United had no chance
Till there came a sudden opening—Banger saw it at a glance,

Seized the ball and beat the tackle, sent a shot in very low,
But Bill Sprightly had it covered, though his movements were
so slow:
Fell, and tipped it round the corner with the hand that he had
bent,
Saved a certain equaliser as the final whistle went!

The cheers rang through the valley as the players gathered
round
And put Bill on their shoulders as they took him from the
ground.
It was only two hours later, when the local doctor spoke,
They knew that Bill's last save was made with an ELBOW
THAT WAS BROKE!

Neil Adams

74   To-day

So here hath been dawning
Another blue day:
Think, wilt thou let it
Slip useless away?

Out of Eternity
This new day is born:
In to Eternity
At night will return.

Behold it aforetime
No eye ever did:
So soon it for ever
From all eyes is hid.

Here hath been dawning
Another blue day:
Think, wilt thou let it
Slip useless away?

Thomas Carlyle

75 Crow and Fox

How often have they told us, please,
And always to no use—that flattery's mean and base?
The flatterer in our hearts will always find a place.
God somehow sent the crow a little piece of cheese.
The crow had perched upon a fir.
She seemed to have settled down to enjoy her provender,
But mused with mouth half-closed, the dainty bit still in it.
Unhappily the fox came running by that minute:
A whiff of scent soon brings him to a pause,
And Reynard sights the cheese, and Reynard licks his jaws.
The rascal steals on tip-toe to the tree,
He curls his tail, and, gazing earnestly,
He speaks so soft, scarce whispering each word:
'How beautiful you are, sweet bird!
What a neck, and oh! what eyes.
Like a dream of Paradise!
Then, what feathers! what a beak!
And, sure, an angel's voice if only you would speak!
Sing, darling; don't be shy! Oh, sister, truth to tell,
If you, with charms like these, can sing as well,
Of birds you'd be the queen adorable!
The silly creature's head turns giddy with his praise;
Her breath, for very rapture, swells her throat;
The fox's soft persuasion she obeys,
And high as a crow can pitch she caws one piercing note.
Down falls the cheese! Both cheese and fox have gone their
ways.

Krylov (translated from the Russian by Bernard Pares)

76 Home?

'Yes, we have a home,
But no house to put round it.'

Comment by a child of refugee parents

77   The Shooting of Dan McGrew

A bunch of the boys were whooping it up in the Malamute
        saloon;
The kid that handles the music-box was hitting a rag-time tune;
Back of the bar, in a solo game, sat Dangerous Dan McGrew,
And watching his luck was his light-o'-love, the lady that's
        known as Lou.

When out of the night, which was fifty below, and into the din
        and the glare,
There stumbled a miner fresh from the creeks, dog-dirty and
        loaded for bear.
He looked like a man with a foot in the grave, and scarcely
        the strength of a louse,
Yet he tilted a poke of dust on the bar, and he called for
        drinks on the house.
There was none could place the stranger's face, though we
        searched ourselves for a clue;
But we drank his health, and the last to drink was Dangerous
        Dan McGrew.

There's men that somehow just grip your eyes, and hold them
        hard like a spell;
And such was he, and he looked to me like a man who had
        lived in hell;
With a face most hair, and the dreary stare of a dog whose
        day is done,
As he watered the green stuff in his glass, and the drops
        fell one by one.

Then I got to figgering who he was, and wondering what
        he'd do,
And I turned my head—and there watching him was the lady
        that's known as Lou.

His eyes went rubbering round the room, and he seemed in
        a kind of daze,
Till at last the old piano fell in the way of his wandering
        gaze.

The rag-time kid was having a drink; there was no one else
        on the stool,
So the stranger stumbles across the room, and flops down there
        like a fool.
In a buckskin shirt that was glazed with dirt he sat, and I
        saw him sway;
Then he clutched the keys with his talon hands—my God! but
        that man could play!

Were you ever out in the Great Alone, when the moon was
        awful clear,
And the icy mountains hemmed you in with a silence you 'most
        could hear;
With only the howl of a timber wolf, and you camped there in
        the cold,
A half-dead thing in a stark, dead world, clean mad for the
        muck called gold;
While high overhead, green, yellow, and red, the North Lights
        swept in bars—
Then you've a hunch what the music meant . . . hunger and
        night and the stars.

And hunger not of the belly kind, that's banished with bacon
        and beans;
But the gnawing hunger of lonely men for a home and all that
        it means;
For a fireside far from the cares that are, four walls and
        a roof above;
But oh! so cramful of cosy joy, and crowned with a woman's
        love;
A woman dearer than all the world, and true as Heaven is
        true—
(God! how ghastly she looks through her rouge—the lady
        that's known as Lou.)

Then on a sudden the music changed, so soft that you scarce
        could hear;
But you felt that your life had been looted clean of all that
        it once held dear;
That someone had stolen the women you loved; that her love
        was a devil's lie;

That your guts were gone, and the best for you was to crawl
    away and die.
'Twas the crowning cry of a heart's despair, and it thrilled
    you through and through—
'I guess I'll make it a spread misere,' said Dangerous Dan
    McGrew.

The music almost died away . . . then it burst like a pent-up
    flood;
And it seemed to say, 'Repay, repay,' and my eyes were blind
    with blood.
The thought came back of an ancient wrong, and it stung like
    a frozen lash,
And the lust awoke to kill, to kill . . . then the music
    stopped with a crash,

And the stranger turned, and his eyes they burned in a most
    peculiar way;
In a buckskin shirt that was glazed with dirt he sat, and I
    saw him sway;
Then his lips went in in a kind of grin, and he spoke, and
    his voice was calm;
And, 'Boys,' says he, 'you don't know me, and none of you
    care a damn;
But I want to state, and my words are straight, and I'll
    bet my poke they're true,
That one of you is a hound of hell . . . and that one is
    Dan McGrew.'

Then I ducked my head, and the lights went out, and two
    guns blazed in the dark;
And a woman screamed, and the lights went up, and two men
    lay stiff and stark;
Pitched on his head, and pumped full of lead, was Dangerous
    Dan McGrew,
While the man from the creeks lay clutched to the breast of
    the lady that's known as Lou.

These are the simple facts of the case, and I guess I ought
      to know;
They say that the stranger was crazed with 'hooch', and I'm
      not denying it's so.
I'm not so wise as the lawyer guys, but strictly between
      us two—
The woman that kissed him—and pinched his poke—was the
      lady that's known as Lou.

Robert W. Service

78 Rythm

They dunno how it is. I smack a ball
right through the goals. But they dunno how the words
get muddled in my head, get tired somehow.
I look through the window see. And there's a wall
I'd kick the ball against, just smack and smack.
Old Jerry he can't play, he don't know how,
not now at any rate. He's too flicking small.
See him in shorts, out in the crazy black.
Rythm, he says, and ryme. See him at back.
He don't know nuthing about Law. He'd fall
flat on his face, just like a big sack,
when you're going down the wing, the wind behind you
and crossing into the goalmouth and they're roaring
the whole great crowd. They're up on their feet cheering.
The ball's at your feet and there it goes, just crack.
Old Jerry dives—the wrong way. And they're jearing
and I run to the centre and old Bash
jumps up and down, and I feel great, and wearing
my gold and purpel strip, fresh from the wash.

Iain Crichton Smith

79 The People Upstairs

The people upstairs all practise ballet.
Their living room is a bowling alley.
Their bedroom is full of conducted tours.
Their radio is louder than yours.
They celebrate week-ends all the week.
When they take a shower your ceilings leak.
They try to get their parties to mix
By supplying their guests with Pogo sticks,
And when their orgy at last abates,
They go to the bathroom on roller skates.
I might love the people upstairs wondrous
If instead of above us, they just lived under us.

Ogden Nash

80 Middle Ages

I heard a clash, and a cry,
And a horseman fleeing the wood.
The moon hid in a cloud.
Deep in shadow I stood.
'Ugly work!' thought I,
Holding my breath.
'Men must be cruel and proud,
Jousting for death.'

With gusty glimmering shone
The moon; and the wind blew colder.
A man went over the hill,
Bent to his horse's shoulder.

'Time for me to be gone' . . .
Darkly I fled.
Owls in the wood were shrill,
And the moon sank red.

Siegfried Sassoon

81 Georgetown Children

Under the soursop silver-leaf tree
The High School children play skip-and-free:

Sun burning down like a fire ball.
Watch the children before school call

Laugh in their gay time, laughter rich,
Jump the jack, bring marble pitch.

Black child, yellow child, brown child, white,
They are all the same if you looking right.

Pass by any schoolyard in Georgetown stall
And watch the children before school call;

Under the soursop silver-leaf tree
The High School children play skip-and-free.

The biggest thing in life could be
Watching the children play skip-and-free.

Ian Macdonald (Guyana)

82 A Windy Night

As I lie snugly in my bed
I hear the door bang on the shed,
Howling wind and driving rain
The leaves are rattling against the pane.
Outside the sky is turning black
And creepy shivers go down your back.
The stars no longer shine their light,
The clouds are hiding the moon so bright.
A dustbin lid rolls down the path
And the fire is flickering in the hearth.

Gillian (aged 8)

83   Who?

Who is that child I see wandering, wandering
Down by the side of the quivering stream?
Why does he seem not to hear, though I call to him?
Where does he come from, and what is his name?

Why do I see him at sunrise and sunset
Taking, in old fashioned clothes, the same track?
Why, when he walks, does he cast not a shadow
Though the sun rises and falls at his back?

Why does the dust lie so thick on the hedgerow
By the great field where a horse pulls the plough?
Why do I see only meadows, where houses
Stand in a line by the riverside now?

Why does he move like a wraith by the water,
Soft as the thistledown on the breeze blown?
When I draw near him so that I may hear him,
Why does he say that his name is my own?

Charles Causley

84   The Witches' Chant

Double, double, toil and trouble;
Fire, burn; and cauldron, bubble!
> Fillet of fenny snake,
> In the cauldron boil and bake;
> Eye of newt, and toe of frog,
> Wool of bat, and tongue of dog,
> Adder's fork, and blind-worm's sting,
> Lizard's leg, and howlet's wing:
> For a charm of powerful trouble,
> Like a hell-broth boil and bubble.
Double, double, toil and trouble,
Fire burn! and cauldron, bubble!

William Shakespeare. From Macbeth *IV 1*

85   One More Step

One more step along the world I go,
One more step along the world I go.
From the old things to the new,
Keep me travelling along with you.
> And it's from the old I travel to the new.
> Keep me travelling along with you.

Round the corners of the world I turn,
More and more about the world I learn.
All the new things that I see
You'll be looking at along with me.
> And it's from the old I travel to the new.
> Keep me travelling along with you.

As I travel through the bad and good
Keep me travelling the way I should.
Where I see no way to go
You'll be telling me the way I know.
> And it's from the old I travel to the new.
> Keep me travelling along with you.

Give me courage when the world is rough,
Keep me loving though the world is tough.
Leap and sing in all I do,
Keep me travelling along with you.
> And it's from the old I travel to the new.
> Keep me travelling along with you.

You are older than the world can be,
You are younger than the life in me.
Ever old and ever new,
Keep me travelling along with you.
> And it's from the old I travel to the new.
> Keep me travelling along with you.

Sydney Carter

86 Maths Gone Wrong

Think of a sum to show
Bread and people.
How much of one
        for
How many of the other.
For the South American
It's one slice per person.
Fair enough. For the Middle East too.
In Africa, half is the ration.
Two people one slice.
In Europe and Russia
And the States
There's more than plenty.
For every five
There's twelve slices of bread.
But what about Asia?
Not even half
For every eleven
There's just
One
Two
Three
Four
Five
Slices of bread.

Geoffrey Simpson

This poem was inspired by some Save the Children statistics on world food figures. The 'slices of bread' are of course symbolic, but the poem can be enacted very successfully.

87 News

Although the world is full of suffering,
It is also full of overcoming it.

Helen Keller

88   Oats and Beans

Oats and beans and barley grow
Oats and beans and barley grow
Nor you nor I nor anyone know
How oats and beans and barley grow.

First the farmer sows the seed
Then he stands and takes his ease
He stamps his foot and claps his hand
And turns round to view the land.

Waiting for a partner,
Waiting for a partner,
Open the ring and take one in
And bring her to the centre.

Now you're married you must obey
You must be true in all you say
You must be kind, you must be good
And help your wife to chop the wood.

Traditional children's singing game

89   The Knight's Prayer

God be in my head
              And in my understanding;

God be in mine eyes
              And in my looking;

God be in my mouth
              And in my speaking;

God be in my heart
              And in my thinking;

God be at my end
              And at my departing.

Anon

90 Giving

We sing:
>
> Take my life
>
> Take my silver
>
> Take my gold.

But withhold:
>
> All but our small change.

Adapted from an anonymous Indian contribution to a church magazine

91 Harvest Hymn

We spray the fields and scatter
The poison on the ground
So that no wicked wild flowers
Upon our farm be found.
We like whatever helps us
To line our purse with pence;
The twenty-four-hour broiler house
And neat electric fence.

> All concrete sheds around us
> and Jaguars in the yard,
> The telly lounge and deep freeze
> Are ours from working hard.

We fire the fields for harvest,
The hedges swell the flame,
The oak trees and the cottages
From which our fathers came.
We give no compensation,
The earth is ours today,
And if we lose on arable,
The bungalows will pay.

> All concrete sheds around us *etc.*

John Betjeman

92   Song of the Battery Hen

We can't grumble about accommodation:
we have a new concrete floor that's
always dry, four walls that are
painted white, and a sheet-iron roof
the rain drums on. A fan blows warm air
beneath our feet to disperse the smell
of chicken-shit and, on dull days,
fluorescent lighting sees us.

You can tell me: if you come by
the North door, I am in the twelfth pen
on the left hand side of the third row
from the floor; and in that pen
I am usually the middle one of three.
But, even without directions, you'd
discover me. I have the same orange-
red comb, yellow beak and auburn
feathers, but as the door opens and you
hear above the electric fan a kind of
one word wail, I am the one
who sounds loudest in my head.

Listen. Outside this house there's an
orchard with small moss-green apple
trees; beyond that, two fields of
cabbages; then, on the far side of
the road, a broiler house. Listen:
one cockerel crows out there, as
tall and proud as the first hour of the sun.
Sometimes I stop calling with the others
to listen, and wonder if he hears me.

The next time you come here, look for me.
Notice the way I sound inside my head.
God made us all quite differently,
and blessed us with this expensive home.

Edwin Brock

93 The Creator, or How to Make a World

For just one minute before they come
        I lie in my bed
and hear the rain go grumbling round
and round the roof. How awkward it is
for someone who wants to make a world
        and needs to go out
and look for things he knows would help

to get it done! I have to think
        of a way to work
with what's in my head. So I burrow down
like an ant-lion, and make ideas
come tumbling into my woolly trap.
I wrap them round
with a warm cocoon. They have to be good

or I eat them up. Now I shall need
        a lot of wood
and water and grass. I shall need seas
to put fish in. And a flat plain
for cheetah and deer. Two or three warm
        caves for bats
and a nest for owls. And a tree for bears.

Bears like a tree. Bears know how
        to sharpen their claws
on a hairy bark. They steal from bees.
Rabbits can live in a tree, too.
Will one do? I wonder if
        there had better be two?
A pair of trees and a cool pool

for a knowing toad. Under the sea
                there are beetles that dive
and take a bubble down to breathe,
I hear. I have to come up for air.
How cold it is! I shall have to make
                it warmer than this
in my world, or the Mexican dogs

will all be dead. I ought to be neat
                and make my world
a day at a time, but I haven't a day.
I only have twenty seconds before
they come with a drink to make me sleep
                and not even think
for about twelve hours. I shall have to hurry

to get it done. These birds and fish
                that I have to make
from clay and grass must all be quick
and hop or flip into air and pools
as soon as they can. They can squawk and plop
                their balloon-like cheeks
as much as they like. I have to go on

and do the mammals like sloths and stoats
                and whales and cows
and be quick about it. If I have time
I want to make a special beast
with a cold nose and a warm tail
                tucked under its legs
that will learn to sleep and do what I say

when I tell it to. I hear it grunt,
                say, thank you, yes,
and roll itself in a proper ball
beside my chest of drawers. And soon
with a slurping sound to gulp its drink
                it will fall asleep
in its warm bed, it will fall asleep . . .

George Macbeth

94   The Rabbit

We are going to see the rabbit.
We are going to see the rabbit.
Which rabbit, people say?
Which rabbit, ask the children?
Which rabbit?
The only rabbit,
The only rabbit in England,
Sitting behind a barbed wire fence
Under the floodlights, neon lights,
Sodium lights,
Nibbling grass
On the only patch of grass
In England, in England
(Except the grass by the hoardings
Which doesn't count.)
We are going to see the rabbit
And we must be there on time.

First we shall go by escalator,
Then we shall go by underground,
and then we shall go by motorway
And then by helicopterway,
And the last ten yards we shall have to go
On foot.

And now we are going
All the way to see the rabbit,
We are nearly there,
We are longing to see it,
And so is the crowd
Which is here in thousands
With mounted policemen
And big loudspeakers
And bands and banners,
And everyone has come a long way.
But soon we shall see it
Sitting and nibbling
The blades of grass

On the only patch of grass
In—but something has gone wrong!
Why is everyone so angry,
Why is everyone jostling
And slanging and complaining?

The rabbit has gone,
Yes, the rabbit has gone.
He has actually burrowed down into the earth
And made himself a warren, under the earth,
Despite all these people.
And what shall we do?
What can we do?

It is all a pity, you must be disappointed,
Go home and do something else for today,
Go home again, go home for today.
For you cannot hear the rabbit, under the earth,
Remarking rather sadly to himself, by himself,
As he rests in his warren, under the earth:
'It won't be long, they are bound to come,
They are bound to come and find me, even here.'

Alan Brownjohn

95   A Dormitory Suburb

'Will it rain?'
'Do the rose trees need pruning?'
Oh, infinitesimal trivialities!
Does it matter?
Oh, God, is it important?
Nature, tender the rose trees.

If I stood a starving child before you,
I think you would say:
'Ah, poor thing,'
And go on clipping your hedge.

Jenny Scott

96 Schoolmistress

Straight-backed as a Windsor chair
She stood on the top playground step
And surveyed her Saturnalian kingdom.
At eight forty five precisely, she stiffened
(If that were possible), produced a key
—A large, cold dungeon-key—
Placed it below her lip, and blew,
No summons from Heaven itself
(It was a church school) was more imperious!
No angel trumpet or Mosean thunder-clap
Calling the Israelites to doom or repentance
Met swifter obedience. No Gorgon
Suspended life with such efficiency.
In the middle of a shout, a scream,
We halted. Our faces froze.
No longer George or Tom or Mary,
But forty reproductions of a single child,
Chilled to conformity. We gathered
Like captive troops and, climbing steps,
Received the inspection of her cool eyes,
Willing them away from unwashed necks
Or black ringed fingernails,
But knowing our very thoughts were visible
If she chose to see. Nothing escaped her.
She was (as I said, a church school)
God, Saint Michael, the Recording Angel
And, in our guiltier moments, Lucifer—
A Lucifer in long tweed skirts
And a blouse severely fastened at the neck
By a round cameo that was no ornament
But the outward sign of inward authority.

Even the Rector, when he stepped inside
And the brown walls rumbled to his voice,
Dwindled to a curate . . .
It would have astonished us to learn, I think
That she ate supper, went to bed,
And even, perhaps, on occasions, slept.

Clive Sansom

97 Geography Lesson

When the jet sprang into the sky,
it was clear why the city
had developed the way it had,
seeing it scaled six inches to the mile.
There seemed an inevitability
about what on ground had looked haphazard,
unplanned and without style
when the jet sprang into the sky.

When the jet reached ten thousand feet,
it was clear why the country
had cities where rivers ran
and why the valleys were populated.
The logic of geography—
that land and water attracted man—
was clearly delineated
when the jet reached ten thousand feet.

When the jet rose six miles high,
it was clear that the earth was round
and that it had more sea than land.
But it was difficult to understand
that the men on the earth found
causes to hate each other, to build
walls across cities and to kill.
From that height, it was not clear why.

Zulfikar Ghose

98   Lament of the Banana Man

Gal, I'm tellin' you, I'm tired for true,
Tired of Englan', tired o' you.
But I can' go back to Jamaica now . . .

I'm here in Englan', I'm drawin' pay,
I go to de underground every day—
Eight hours is all, half-hour fo' lunch,
M' uniform's free, an' m' ticket punch—
Punchin' tickets not hard to do,
When I'm tired o' punchin', I let dem through.

I get a paid holiday once a year.
Ol' age an' sickness can' touch me here.

I have a room o' m' own, an' an iron bed,
Dunlopillo under m' head,
A Morphy-Richards to warm de air,
A formica table, an easy chair.
I have summer clothes, an' winter clothes,
An' paper kerchiefs to blow m' nose.

My yoke is easy, my burden is light,
I know a place I can go to, any night.
Dis place Englan'! I'm not complainin',
If it col', it col', if it rainin', it rainin'.
I don' min' if it's mostly night,
Dere's always inside, or de sodium light.

I don' min' white people starin' at me
Dey don' want me here? Don't is deir country?
You won' catch me bawlin' any homesick tears
If I don' see Jamaica for a t'ousand years!

. . . Gal, I'm tellin' you, I'm tired fo' true,
Tired of Englan', tired o' you,
I can' go back to Jamaica now—
But I'd want to die there, anyhow.

Evan Jones

99   Hospital Teacher

Only six years old he said
And would I teach him sums.
Other children, boasting hard,
Showed bandaged head,
or body scarred.
'Look, my eye's stitched up.'
'My tummy's cut.'
'Adding sums,' he said.

I stood amid the clamour,
And marvelled they could turn
Their hurt to such a curious match.
But Brian capped them all.
Alas, no adding sums he needed:
Subtraction his poor due.
His covers proudly thrown amok,
Revealing legs (not two)
But one, and one pathetic stump.
'You can't beat that,' he yelled with glee.
Amid the awful silence added,
'I got it from a 'bus.'

Constance Hale

100   Good Advice

You should:

       think the right thoughts
       do things for a good reason
       speak only the truth
       behave as well as possible
       care for all other living creatures
       be as useful as possible
       not act without thought
       always try your hardest.

An adaptation of the Noble Eightfold Path of Buddhism

101 Rain

One quiet splat
As the rain collided with the window.

Drip by slow drip it fell,
Almost reluctant to leave its soft grey home:
Small round drops appeared as I looked down
To the pavement below.

Almost at once the small quaint pools of rain
Changed into heavy angry bullets,
Firing themselves at the window as if trying
To break the glass.
Big, round grenades, bombing the roof tops,
Making them wet and shiny under the street lamps.

Everywhere, thousands and thousands of
Individual raindrops broke away from the
Clouds and poured down on to the
Unexpecting ground.

One loud continuous noise,
As it fell,
Lavishing itself on psychedelic umbrellas,
And beating at the small fragile flowers.

As suddenly as its anger had flared,
It was gone;
And slowly, kind and gentle,
Pattering rain drove out its angry playmate,
Until finally,
Drop by drop, it stopped.

The large tanks in the sky moved on
And the solitary street was quiet
Once more.

Tina Taylor (aged 16)

102　Boy into Heron

High on a stilt raised bed above the reeds
He lay and watched the birds, saw the grey heron come,
Perched like himself on long stiff legs,
To search the mud wet shore for frogs and fish,
Marked his smooth plumage and the deep slate tail,
And the dark coronet of glossy plumes,
And watching so intently, lost himself,
His own identity merged in the birds.
So when the heron rose above the loch,
His thin legs arrowed in the wind,
His plumes laid flat, the boy took wings,
And rose with him and skimmed across the lake
And knew the majesty and joy of flight.
Not till the heron grew a distant speck
Beyond his sight, did he, reluctant, creep
Into his body's wingless form again.

Celia Randall

103　Done For

Old Ben Bailey
He's been and done
For a small brown bunny
With his long gun.

Glazed are the eyes
That stared so clear,
And no sound stirs
In that hairy ear.

What was once beautiful
Now breathes not,
Bound for Ben Bailey's
Smoking pot.

Walter de la Mare

104 Paper Boats

Day by day I float my paper boats one by one
          down the running stream.
In big black letters I write my name on them
          and the name of the village where I live.
I hope that someone in some strange land
          will find them and know who I am.

Rabindranath Tagore

105 The Parting

I pay my last respects,
to you,
Whom I loved so much,
words can not describe
just,—how much.
Throwing the blood red rose,
on to you, lying peacefully
encased in wood,
At last it's over,
The tears flow freely,
falling,
tears over tears.
I think of the cruel words
that I used to say,
The hurtful things.
Why did you have to die
Without knowing
just,—how sorry I am?
Words are useless
Mum,—how sad and lonely
I am,—here without you.

Elaine Wilkinson (aged 14)

106   Wisdom? Understanding?

But tell me, where does wisdom come from?
Where is understanding to be found?
The road to it is still unknown to man,
not to be found in the land of the living.
'It is not in me,' says the Abyss;
'Nor here,' replies the Sea.
It cannot be bought with solid gold,
Nor paid for with any weight of silver,
nor be priced by the standard of the gold of Ophir,
or of precious onyx or sapphire.
No gold, no glass can match it in value,
nor for a fine gold vase can it be bartered.
Nor is there need to mention coral, nor crystal;
beside wisdom pearls are not worth the fishing.
Topaz from Cush is worthless in comparison,
and gold, even refined, is valueless.
But tell me where does wisdom come from?
Where is understanding to be found?
Is it outside the knowledge of every living thing,
Hidden from the birds in the sky?
Perdition and death can only say,
'We have heard reports of it.'
God alone has traced its path
and found out where it lives.
(For he sees to the ends of the earth,
and observes all that lies under heaven.)
When he willed to give weight to the wind
and measured out the waters with a gauge,
when he made the laws and rules for the rain
and mapped a route for thunderclaps to follow,
then he had it in sight, and cast its worth,
assessed it, fathomed it.
And he said to man,
'Wisdom? It is the fear of the Lord.
Understanding? Avoidance of Evil.'

Job XXVIII 12–28

107 Housing

Lord, I can't sleep; I have got up out of bed to pray.
It is night outside, and the wind blows and the rain falls.
And the lights of the city, signs of the living, pierce the
    darkness.
They bother me, Lord, these lights—why are you showing
    them to me?
They beckoned to me, and now they hold me captive, while the
    woes of the city murmur their muffled lament.

And I cannot escape them, Lord; I know these sufferings too
    well.
I see them rising before me,
I hear them speaking to me,
I feel them hitting me,
They were bothering me when I was trying to sleep.

I know that in one single room thirteen crowded people are
    breathing on one another.
I know a mother who hooks the table and the chairs to the
    ceiling to make room for mattresses.
I know that rats come out to eat the crusts and bite the babies.
I know a father who gets up to stretch oil-cloth above the rain-
    soaked bed of his four children.
I know a mother who stays up all night since there is room for
    only one bed, and the two children are sick.
I know a drunken father who vomits on the child sleeping
    beside him.
I know a big boy who runs away alone into the night because
    he can't stand it any more.
I know that some men fight for the women as there are three
    couples in the same attic.
I know a wife who avoids her husband as there is no room for
    another baby at home.
I know a child who is quietly dying, soon to join his four little
    brothers above.

I know . . .
I know hundreds of others—yet I was going to sleep peacefully
     between my clean white sheets.

I wish I didn't know, Lord.
I wish it were not true.
I wish I could convince myself that I'm dreaming,
I wish someone could prove that I'm exaggerating,
I wish they'd show me that all these people are to blame, that
     it's their fault that they are so miserable.
I'd like to be reassured, Lord, but I can't, it's too late.
I've seen too much,
I've listened too much,
I've counted too much, and, Lord, these ruthless figures have
     robbed me forever of my innocent tranquillity.

So much the better, son,
For I, your God, your Father, am angry with you.
I gave you the world at the beginning of time, and I want each
            of my sons to have a home worthy of their Father,
            in my vast kingdom.
I trusted you, and your selfishness has spoiled everything.
It's one of your most serious sins, shared by many of you.
Woe unto you if, through your fault, a single one of my sons
            dies in body or in spirit.

I tell you, I will give to those the finest lodgings in Paradise.
But the thoughtless, the negligent, the selfish, who, well
            sheltered on earth, have forgotten others, they
            have had their reward.
There will be no room for them in my Kingdom.

Come, son, ask forgiveness for yourself and for others tonight.
And tomorrow, fight with all your strength, for it hurts your
            Father to see that once more there is no more room
            his son at the inn.

Michel Quoist

108 Days

What are days for?
Days are where we live.
They come, they wake us
Time and time over.
They are to be happy in:
Where can we live but days?

Ah, solving that question
Brings the priest and the doctor
In their long coats
Running over the fields.

Philip Larkin

109 Good Advice

With coarse food to eat,
Water to drink,
And a bent arm for a pillow,
Happiness may still be found.

Confucius

110 The Ordinary Man

If you and I should chance to meet,
I guess you wouldn't care;
I'm sure you'd pass me in the street
As if I wasn't there;
You'd never look me in the face,
My modest mug to scan,
Because I'm just a commonplace
      And Ordinary Man.

But then, it may be, you are too
A guy of every day,
Who does the job he's told to do
And takes the wife his pay;
Who makes a home and kids his care,
And works with pick or pen . . .
Why, Pal, I guess we're just a pair
      Of Ordinary Men.

We plug away and make no fuss,
Our feats are never crowned;
And yet it's common coves like us
Who make the world go round.
And as we steer a steady course
By God's predestined plan,
Hats off to that almighty Force:
      THE ORDINARY MAN.

Robert Service

111   Black, Brown and White

Just listen to the song I'm singin', brother,
You'll know it's true.
If you're black and got to work for a livin', boy,
This is what they'll say to you:
> Now if you're white, you're right
> And if you're brown, stick around,
> But if you're black, O brother,
> Get back, get back, get back.

I 'member I was in a place one night,
Everybody was having fun,
They was all drinking beer and wine,
But me I couldn't get none.
> Now if you're white, you're right
> And if you're brown, stick around,
> But if you're black, O brother,
> Get back, get back, get back.

I was in an employment office,
I got a number and got in line.
They called out everybody's number
But they never did call mine.
> Now if you're white, you're right
> And if you're brown, stick around,
> But if you're black, O brother,
> Get back, get back, get back.

Me and a man was workin' side by side,
And this is what it meant.
He was gettin' a dollar an hour
And I was gettin' fifty cent.
> Now if you're white, you're right
> And if you're brown, stick around,
> But if you're black, O brother,
> Get back, get back, get back.

I helped build this country,
I fought for it too,
Now what I want to know is,
What you gonna do about Jim Crow?

>Now if you're white, you're right
>And if you're brown, stick around,
>But if you're black, O brother,
>Get back, get back, get back.

Big Bill Broonzy

112 Our Mother

Hundreds of stars in the pretty sky,
Hundreds of shells on the shore together,
Hundreds of birds that go singing by,
Hundreds of birds in the sunny weather.

Hundreds of dewdrops to greet the dawn,
Hundreds of bees in the purple clover,
Hundreds of butterflies on the lawn,
But only one mother the wide world over.

Anon

113 Words

When you think about words
Its not long before
You know that
Some are
Sad.
The one
I think is
The saddest of all
Is
ONLY.

Andrew (aged 9)

114   At the Fair

Yellow lights, blue lights,
Flickering and beaming,
Pop music blaring out
People shouting,
Happy faces all about me.
As I walked along dodging a couple of people
I watched others putting money in
A slot machine.
Then the excited faces as money
Fell out into their hands.
Children laughed as they whizzed down the helta skelta
But I was sad because I had no money,
So all I could do was watch
People screaming as they went through the ghost train,
Laughing as they shot down on the dive bombers
And banging with guns at the stalls.
Then suddenly there was more silence than noise.
The fair was closing,
All the lights were going off,
I noticed all the litter lying on the ground.
I went home.

Andrew (aged 9)

115   I will Give my Love an Apple

I will give my love an apple without e're a core,
I will give my love a house without e'er a door,
I will give my love a palace wherein she may be,
And she may unlock it without any key.

My head is the apple without e're a core,
My mind is the house without e'er a door,
My heart is the palace wherein she may be,
And she may unlock it without any key.

Anon

78

116   What Makes Me Me?

What makes me me?
A number of things.
I absolutely hate Chops.
I simply love Sweets.
I loathe Fox Hunting.
I admire Football.
My Girlfriend is attractive.
My Sister is repulsive.
Games are enjoyable.
Work is acceptable.
But Maths is abominable.
So are the Olympics.
I absolutely hate Cauliflower.
I love Ice-Cream.
Is that what makes me me?

Paul Bunch

117   Edinburgh Rain and Love Poem

once in Edinburgh
I had a sudden
urge
to post your letter
down a drain

not because
I was tiring of you

but because

my thoughts should reach you
anyhow

through grates
through orange peel
through dirty water.

Lindsay Levy

118 Casey Jones

Come all you rounders if you want to hear
The story of a brave engineer;
Casey Jones was the hogger's name,
On a big eight-wheeler, boys, he won his fame.
Caller called Casey at half-past four,
He kissed his wife at the station door,
Mounted to the cabin with orders in his hand,
And took his farewell trip to the promised land.

       Casey Jones, he mounted to the cabin,
       Casey Jones, with his orders in his hand!
       Casey Jones, he mounted to the cabin,
       Took his farewell trip into the promised land.

'Put in your water and shovel in your coal,
Put your head out the window, watch the drivers roll,
I'll run her till she leaves the rail,
'Cause we're eight hours late with the Western Mail!'
He looked at his watch and his watch was slow,
Looked at the water and the water was low,
Turned to his fireboy and said,
'We'll get to 'Frisco, but we'll all be dead!'

       Casey Jones, he mounted to the cabin, *etc.*

Casey pulled up Reno Hill,
Tooted for the crossing with an awful shrill,
Snakes all knew by the engine's moans
That the hogger at the throttle was Casey Jones.
He pulled up short two miles from the place,
Number Four stared him right in the face,
Turned to his fireboy, said, 'You'd better jump,
'Cause there's two locomotives that's going to bump.'

       Casey Jones, he mounted to the cabin, *etc.*

Casey said, just before he died,
'There's two more roads I'd like to ride.'
Fireboy said, 'What can they be?'
'The Rio Grande and the Old S.P.'
Mrs Jones sat on her bed a-sighing,
Got a pink that Casey was dying.
Said, 'Go to bed, children; hush your crying,
'Cause you'll get another papa on the Salt Lake line.'

> Casey Jones! Got another papa!
> Casey Jones, on the Salt Lake Line!
> Casey Jones! Got another papa!
> Got another papa on the Salt Lake Line!

Anon

119 Winter

When icicles hang by the wall,
>　　And Dick the shepherd blows his nail,
And Tom bears logs into the hall,
>　　And milk comes frozen home in pail;
When blood is nipped, and ways be foul
Then nightly sings the staring owl
>　　　　Tu-who;
>　　Tu-whit, tu-who—a merry note,
>　　While greasy Joan doth keel the pot.

When all aloud the wind doth blow,
>　　And coughing drowns the parson's saw,
And birds sit brooding in the snow,
>　　And Marian's nose looks red and raw,
When roasted crabs hiss in the bowl,
Then nightly sings the staring owl
>　　　　Tu-who;
>　　Tu-whit, tu-who—a merry note,
>　　While greasy Joan doth keel the pot.

William Shakespeare

120   School's Out

Girls scream,
> Boys shout;
Dogs bark,
> School's out.

Cats run,
> Horses shy;
Into trees
> Birds fly.

Babes wake
> Open-eyed;
If they can,
> Tramps hide.

Old man,
> Hobble home;
Merry mites,
> Welcome.

W. H. Davies

121   Look Well

A man has not begun to see
> Who cannot see beneath the snow
The flower destined for the bee,
> The corn that he has yet to sow;
Who cannot see the second side
> To any question argued out
And give the ebbing half of tide
> At least the benefit of doubt.
There should be graven on each stone
> For every simple man to spell
'He sees most clearly through his own
> Who sees through others' eyes as well.'

Anon

122   A Knight Came Riding

A knight came riding from the East,
> Jennifer, gentle and rosemarie,
Who had been wooing at many a place,
> As the dove flies over the mulberry tree.

He came and knocked at the lady's gate,
One evening when it was growing late.

The eldest sister let him in,
And pinned the door with a silver pin.

The second sister, she made his bed
And laid soft pillows under his head.

The youngest sister was bold and bright
And she would wed with this unco' knight.

'If you will answer me questions three,
This very day will I marry thee.

'O what is louder nor a horn?
And what is sharper nor a thorn?

'What is heavier nor the lead?
And what is better nor the bread?

'O what is higher nor the tree?
And what is deeper nor the sea?'

'O, shame is louder nor a horn,
And hunger sharper nor a thorn.

'A sin is heavier nor the lead,
And the blessing's better nor the bread.

'O, Heaven is higher nor the tree,
And love is deeper nor the sea.'

'O, you have answered my questions three,
> Jennifer, gentle and rosemarie,
And so, fair maid, I'll marry with thee,
> As the dove flies over the mulberry tree.'

Anon

123 Hunger

Voice 1 Whose are the voices crying, crying?
Whose are the pitiful pleas we hear?
Whose is the sorrow that finds tongue in weeping?
Whose hopelessness speaks with despair?

Voice 2 Ours are the voices crying, crying;
Ours are the pitiful pleas you hear.
We are the people you hear at our weeping
Ours is the empty cry of despair.

Voice 1 Whose are the faces so drawn with suffering?
Whose are the bodies no more than bones?
Whose are the eyes that are hopeless and lifeless?
Whose are the graves with nameless stones?

Voice 2 Ours are the faces gaunt with starvation.
Ours are the wasted dying frames.
Ours are the hungry eyes of the hopeless,
Ours are the graves with no names.

Voice 1 Why do I hear your cries of starvation?
Why show me hunger I don't wish to see?
Why are your skeleton fingers still reaching
Endlessly, endlessly out to me?

Voice 2 Have we been changed so much by our suffering?
In our extremity aren't we the same?
Brother to brother, we reach out our hands to you
Flesh of one flesh are we, name of one name.

Voice 1 What can I do for you brother, my brother?
How can I help? I am too far away.
Leave it to God, hungry brother, my brother,
Go down on your thin starving knees, and pray.

Voice 2 We have prayed distant brother with fierce
            desperation—

Voice 1 Has God in His Mercy shown what you must do?

Voice 2 He has, brother, answered our earnest entreaties,
He has answered our prayers and his answer is
                    YOU.

Anon

124   Goodbat Nightman

God bless all policemen
and fighters of crime,
May thieves go to jail
for a very long time.

They've had a hard day
helping clean up the town,
Now they hang from the mantelpiece
both upside down.

A glass of warm blood
and then straight up the stairs,
Batman and Robin
are saying their prayers.

They've locked all the doors
and they've put out the bat,
Put on their batjamas
(They like doing that.)

They've filled their batwater-bottles
made their batbeds,
With two springy battresses
for sleepy batheads.

They're closing red eyes
and they're counting black sheep,
Batman and Robin
are falling asleep.

Roger McGough

125 The Key of the Kingdom

When we were children
We possessed the key to a kingdom
Such as this world has yet to see.
Wherever we went;
By lakes,
Pools
And streams,
In woods,
Meadows
And fields,
There was a world beyond belief
In which anything could be something else.
A world
Whose every corner
Would yield some new adventure or surprise.
A world
In which we ruled
And was ours alone.

Only we children had the key,
The key of the kingdom.

A world inhabited by goblins, ghosts and ghouls,
Dragons, trolls, witches, sorcerers,
Knights, fair damsels, wicked kings
And green skinned, three eyed floops.
A world of enchanted geography—
Magic forests,
Glass mountains
And fountains of youth.

Ed Reed

126   Leave Her, Johnny

Oh, the times are hard and the wages low—
        Leave her, Johnny, leave her.
And now ashore again we'll go—
        It's time for us to leave her.

The grub was bad, the voyage long—
        Leave her, Johnny, leave her.
The seas were high, the gales were strong—
        It's time for us to leave her.

She would not wear, she would not stay—
        Leave her, Johnny, leave her.
She shipped it green both night and day—
        It's time for us to leave her.

She would not stay, she would not wear—
        Leave her, Johnny, leave her.
She shipped it green and she made us swear—
        It's time for us to leave her.

The sails are furled, our work is done—
        Leave her, Johnny, leave her.
And now ashore we'll take a run—
        It's time for us to leave her.

Anon

127 New Houses, New Clothes

New houses, new furniture, new streets,
      new clothes, new sheets
everything new and machine-made sucks life out of us
and makes us cold, makes us lifeless
the more we have.

D. H. Lawrence

128 Growing Pain

The boy was barely five years old.
We sent him to the little school
And left him there to learn the names
Of flowers in jam jars on the sill,
And learn to do as he was told.
He seemed quite happy there until
Three weeks afterwards, at night,
The darkness whimpered in his room.
I went upstairs, switched on his light,
And found him wideawake, distraught,
Sheets mangled and his eiderdown an
Untidy carpet on the floor.
I said, 'Why can't you sleep? A pain?'
He snuffled, gave a little moan,
And then he spoke a single word,
'Jessica.' The sound was blurred.
'Jessica? What do you mean?'
'A girl at school called Jessica,
She hurts.' He touched himself between
The heart and stomach, 'and she has been
Aching here and I can see her.'
Nothing I had heard or read
Instructed me in what to do.
I covered him and stroked his head.
'The pain will go, in time,' I said.

Vernon Scannell

129 Autumn

When the slow moving birds
Begin their seasonal flight,
Picked like witches' entrails
Against the dying sky,
Man, seduced by transient colour,
Retreats into memories of
Summer, warmth and sun.

Redvers Brandling

130 An Indian Summer on the Prairie

IN THE BEGINNING
The sun is a huntress young,
The sun is a red, red joy,
The sun is an Indian girl,
Of the tribe of the Illinois.

MID MORNING
The sun is a smouldering fire,
That creeps through the high grey plain;
That leaves not a bush of cloud
To blossom with flowers of rain.

NOON
The sun is a wounded deer,
That treads pale grass in the skies,
Shaking his golden horns,
Flashing his baleful eyes.

SUNSET
The sun is an eagle old,
There in the windless west.
Atop of the spirit-cliffs
He builds him a crimson nest.

Vachel Lindsay

131 Times

To every thing there is a season,
And a time to every purpose under the heaven;
    A time to be born,
        And a time to die;
    A time to plant,
        And a time to pluck up that which is
        planted . . .
    A time to break down,
        And a time to build up;
    A time to weep,
        And a time to laugh;
    A time to mourn,
        And a time to dance;
    A time to cast away stones,
        And a time to gather stones together;
    A time to embrace,
        And a time to refrain from embracing;
    A time to get,
        And a time to lose;
    A time to keep,
        And a time to cast away;
    A time to rend,
        And a time to sew;
    A time to keep silence,
        And a time to speak . . .

Ecclesiastes III 1–7

132 Enough

It does not matter that my house is rather small;
One cannot sleep in more than one room!
It does not matter that I have not many horses;
One cannot ride on two horses at once!

Po Chü-i

90

133 A Thought

Remember
that
Today
is the very first day
of the rest of your
Life.

Anon

134   The Prayer of the Donkey

O God who made me
to trudge along the road
always,
to carry heavy loads
and to be beaten
always!
Give me great courage and gentleness
One day let somebody understand me
that I may no longer want to weep
because I can never say what I mean
and they make fun of me.
Let me find a juicy thistle—
and make them give me time to pick it.
And, Lord, one day let me find again
my little brother of the Christmas crib.

                              Amen.

Rumer Godden

135   The Lonely Scarecrow

My poor old bones—I've only two—
A broomshank and a broken stave,
My ragged gloves are a disgrace,
My one peg-foot is in the grave.

I wear the labourer's old clothes;
Coat, shirt and trousers all undone.
I bear my cross upon a hill
In rain and shine, in snow and sun.

I cannot help the way I look,
My funny hat is full of hay
—O wild birds, come and rest in me!
Why do you always fly away?

James Kirkup

136   The Long Ago Boy

Sometimes I meet the boy I was. He's the colour
Of lightning. He leads me
Between stoat tracks, smudged
With bright blood, in the snow
He juggles with snowballs.

That long ago boy lolls also in hollow oak
Out of the sleet, and counts dead leaves
Like winnings. Up to his chin he is
In rusty guineas. He'll sniff
The pinesmoke in the candlelight
And the air on the green hill
Glorified with snow.

My long ago boy has been busy tasting the frost
Spun like candy floss about
The spikes of a buckled bike.
And he's sucked the icicles
That bristle from the eaves, and licked
The tongues sticking out of milk bottles.

The boy's ribs are bruised
By the bullying northpaw wind.
When he weeps, it's hailstones.
When he laughs, the loch gets gooseflesh.
The sun is bleeding to death in a puddle of slush.
O long ago boy let's spit at it. Tonight
We'll claw all the stars down
That dangle from Orion's stupid belt.

Robert Nye

137   The Frog and the Crow

A jolly fat frog did in the river swim, O.
A comely black crow lived on the river brim, O.
'Come on ashore, come on ashore,' said the crow to the frog,
       and then, O.
'No you'll bite me; you'll bite me,' said the fog to the
       crow again, O.

'Oh there is sweet music on yonder green hill, O.
And you shall be a dancer, a dancer in yellow.
All in yellow, all in yellow,' said the crow to the frog, and
       then, O.
'All in yellow, all in yellow,' said the frog to the crow again, O.

'Farewell, ye little fishes, that in the river swim, O.
I go to be a dancer, a dancer in yellow.'
'Oh, beware; oh beware,' said the fish to the frog and then, O.
'I'll take care, I'll take care,' said the frog to the fish again, O.

The frog began a-swimming, a-swimming to land, O.
The crow began a-hopping to give him his hand, O.
'Sir, you're welcome; sir, you're welcome,' said the crow to the
       frog, and then, O.
'Sir, I thank you; sir, I thank you,' said the frog to the crow
       again, O.

'But where is the music on yonder green hill, O?
And where are all the dancers, the dancers in yellow?
All in yellow, all in yellow,' said the frog to the crow, and
       then, O—
But he chuckled, oh he chuckled, and then O, and then, O!

Anon

138　Hawk

The Hawk looking for something to eat,
The Hawk has eyes like wood chippings,
Hawk flying high in the orange sky.
But there in the wheat;
a Vole.
This is my chance to stab him in the back.
Sharp claws like flint.

Paul Leadbetter (aged 8)

139　The Miller

The Miller, stout and sturdy as the stones
Delighted in his muscles and big bones . . .
He was short shouldered, broad, knotty and tough . . .
Upon the tiptop of his nose he had
A wart, and thereon stood a tuft of hairs,
Bright as the bristles of a red sow's ears . . .

From The Canterbury Tales *by Geoffrey Chaucer*

140　What Kind of Liar Are You?

What kind of liar are you?
People lie because they don't remember clearly what they saw.
People lie because they can't help making a story better than it
was the way it happened.
People tell 'white lies' so as to be decent to others.
People lie in a pinch, hating to do it, but lying on because it
might be worse.
And people lie just to be liars for a crooked personal gain.
What sort of liar are you?
Which of these liars are you?

Carl Sandburg

141 Danny Murphy

He was as old as old could be,
His little eye could hardly see,
His mouth was sunken in between
His nose and chin, and he was lean
And twisted up and withered quite,
So that he couldn't walk aright.

His pipe was always going out,
And then he'd have to search about
In all his pockets, and he'd mow
—O, deary me! and, musha now!
And then he'd light his pipe, and then
He'd let it go clean out again.

He couldn't dance or jump or run,
Or ever have a bit of fun
Like me and Susan, when we shout
And jump and throw ourselves about:
—But when he laughed, then you could see
He was as young as young could be!

James Stephens

142 A Conversation Overheard

No school today?

Oh yes school everyday
we play games and
sing and dance and
say ABC and add and
pray and fight and
paint and cry and laugh.

Do you like school?

No.

Anon

96

143 A Prayer Found in Chester Cathedral

Give me a good digestion, Lord,
   And also something to digest;
Give me a healthy body, Lord,
   With sense to keep it at its best.

Give me a healthy mind, good Lord,
   To keep the good and pure in sight,
Which seeing sin is not appalled
   But finds a way to set it right.

Give me a mind that is not bored,
   That does not whimper, whine or sigh;
Don't let me worry overmuch
   About the fussy thing called I.

Give me a sense of humour, Lord,
   Give me the grace to see a joke,
To get some happiness from life
   And pass it on to other folk.

Anon

144 Night Bombers

Eastward they climb, black shapes against the grey
Of falling dusk, gone with the nodding day
From English fields. Not theirs the sudden glow
Of triumph that their fighter-brothers know;
Only to fly through cloud, through storm, through night,
Unerring, and to keep their purpose bright,
Nor turn until, their dreadful duty done,
Westward they climb to race the awakened sun.

Anon

145 I Share my Bedroom with my Brother

I share my bedroom with my brother
and I don't like it.
His bed's by the window
under my map of England's railways
that has a hole in just above Leicester
where Tony Sanders, he says,
killed a Roman centurion
with the Radio Times.

My bed's in the corner
and the paint on the skirting board
wrinkles when I push it with my thumb
which I do sometimes when I go to bed
sometimes when I wake up
but mostly on Sundays
when we stay in bed all morning.

That's when he makes pillow dens
under the blankets
so that only his left eye shows
and when I go deep-bed mining
for elastoplast spools
that I scatter with my feet
the night before,
and I jump onto his bed
shouting: eeyoueeyoueeyouee
heaping pillows on his head:
'Now breathe, now breathe'
and then there's quiet and silence
so I pull it away quick
and he's there laughing all over
sucking fresh air along his breathing-tube fingers.

Actually, sharing's all right.

Michael Rosen

146　Leisure

What is this life if, full of care,
We have no time to stand and stare?

No time to stand beneath the boughs
And stare as long as sheep or cows.

No time to see, when woods we pass,
Where squirrels hide their nuts in grass.

No time to see, in broad daylight,
Streams full of stars, like skies at night.

No time to turn at Beauty's glance,
And watch her feet, how they can dance.

No time to wait till her mouth can
Enrich that smile her eyes began.

A poor life this if, full of care,
We have no time to stand and stare.

W. H. Davies

147　What is a Friend?

What is a friend?
He could be big or he could be small.
He'll be good to know when you feel sad.
When you want to laugh so will he.
He'll always be ready to share alike.
When others are rude he won't agree.
He'll be the one you're ALWAYS
Glad to see.

From a group of primary children's preparation for a class assembly

148 The Wonderful Words

Never let a thought shrivel and die
For want of a way to say it,
For English is a wonderful game
And all of you can play it.
All that you do is match the words
To the brightest thoughts in your head
So that they come out clear and true
And handsomely groomed and fed—
For many of the loveliest things
Have never yet been said.
Words are the food and dress of thought,
They give it its body and swing,
And everyone's longing today to hear
Some fresh and beautiful thing.
But only words can free a thought
From its prison behind your eyes.
Maybe your mind is holding now
A marvellous new surprise!

Mary O'Neill

149 Justice

On tele
We see programmes about animals
Killing people
For food.

We think this
Terrible.

Frequently forgetting that people
Kill animals
For fun.

Anna Pytlik

150   An Old Woman of the Roads

Oh, to have a little house!
To own the hearth and stool and all!
The heaped-up sods upon the fire,
The pile of turf against the wall!

To have a clock with weights and chains
And pendulum swinging up and down!
A dresser filled with shining delph,
Speckled and white and blue and brown!

I could be busy all the day
Clearing and sweeping hearth and floor,
And fixing up their shelf again
My white and blue and speckled store!

I could be quiet there at night
Beside the fire and by myself,
Sure of a bed and loth to leave
The ticking clock and the shining delph!

Och! but I'm weary of mist and dark,
And roads where there's never a house or bush,
And tired I am of bog and road
And the crying wind and the lonesome hush!

And I am praying to God on high
And I am praying Him night and day,
For a little house—a house of my own—
Out of the wind's and the rain's way.

Padraic Colum

151 Arithmetic

I'm 11. And I don't really know
my Two Times Table. Teacher says it's disgraceful.
But even if I had the time, I feel too tired.
Ron's 5, Samantha's 3, Carole's 18 months,
and then there's Baby. I do what's required.

Mum's working, Dad's away. And so
I dress them, give them breakfast. Mrs Russell
moves in, and I take Ron to school.
Miss Eames calls me an old-fashioned word: Dunce.
Doreen Maloney says I'm a fool.

After tea, to the Rec. Pram-pushing's slow
but on fine days it's a good place, full
of larky boys. When 6 shows on the clock
I put the kids to bed. I'm free for once.
At about 7—Mum's key in the lock.

Gavin Ewart

152 The Little Cart

The little cart jolting and banging through the yellow haze of
        dust
The man pushing behind; the woman pushing in front.
They have left the city and do not know where to go.
'Green, green those elm-tree leaves; they will cure my hunger,
If only we could find some quiet place and sup together.'
The wind had flattened the yellow mother-wort;
Above it in the distance they could see the walls of a house.
'There surely must be people living who'll give you something
        to eat.'
They tap at the door but no-one comes; they'll look in, but the
        kitchen is empty.
They stand hesitating in the lonely road and their fears feel like
        rain.

Anon

153   Two Little Kittens

Two little kittens, one stormy night,
Began to quarrel and then to fight.
One had a mouse, the other had none,
And that's the way the quarrel began.

'I'll have that mouse,' said the bigger cat.
'You'll have that mouse? We'll see about that!'
'I will have that mouse!' said the older one.
'You shan't have that mouse!' said the little one.

I told you before 'twas a stormy night
When those two little kittens began to fight.
The old woman seized her sweeping broom,
And swept the two kittens right out of the room.

The ground was all covered with frost and snow,
And the two little kittens had nowhere to go.
So they laid them down on the mat at the door,
While the old woman finished sweeping the floor.

Then they both crept in as quiet as mice,
All wet with the snow and as cold as ice.
For they found it much better that stormy night
To lie down and sleep, than to quarrel and fight.

Anon

154   A Truth?

What has been

> is

What will be,
And what has been done

> is

What will be done;
And there is nothing new under the sun.

Ecclesiastes I 9

155   Posting Letters

There are no lamps in our village,
And when the owl-and-bat black night
Creeps up low fields
And sidles along the manor walls
I walk quickly.

It is winter;
The letters patter from my hand
Into the tin box in the cottage wall;
The gate taps behind me,
And the road in the sliver of moonlight
Gleams greasily
Where the tractors have stood.

I have to go under the spread fingers of the trees
Under the dark windows of the old man's house,
Where the panes in peeling frames
Flash like spectacles
As I tip-toe.
But there is no sound of him in his one room
In the Queen Anne shell,
Behind the shutters.

I run past the gates,
Their iron feet gaitered with grass,
Into the church porch,
Perhaps for sanctuary,
Standing, hand on the cold door ring,
While above
The tongue-tip of the clock
Clops
Against the hard palate of the tower.

The door groans as I push
And
Dare myself to dash
Along the flagstones to the great brass bird,
To put one shrinking hand
Upon the gritty lid
Of Black Tom's tomb.

Don't tempt whatever spirits stir
In this damp corner,
But
Race down the aisle,
Blunder past font,
Fumble the door,
Leap steps,
Clang iron gate,
And patter through the short-cut muddy lane.

Oh, what a pumping of breath
And choking throat
For three letters.
And now there are the cattle
Stirring in the straw
So close
I can hear their soft muzzling and coughs;
And there are the bungalows,
And the steel-blue miming of the little screen;
And the familiar rattle of the latch,
And our own knocker
Clicking like an old friend;
And
I am home.

Gregory Harrison

156   Tinker's Wife

I saw her amid the dunghill debris
Looking for things
Such as an old pair of shoes or gaiters.
She was a young woman,
A tinker's wife.

Her face had streaks of care
Like wires across it,
But she was supple
As a young goat
On a windy hill.

She searched on the dunghill debris,
Tripping gingerly
Over tin canisters
And sharp-broken
Dinner plates.

Patrick Kavanagh

157

Three things cannot long
        be hidden,
            the sun,
          the moon
      and the truth.

Buddha

158

Do not worry about people
not knowing your ability.
Worry about not having it.

Confucius

159 The Tiger

The tiger behind the bars of his cage growls,
The tiger behind the bars of his cage snarls,
The tiger behind the bars of his cage roars.

Then he thinks.

It would be nice not to be behind bars all
The time
Because they spoil my view.
I wish I were wild, not on show.
But if I were wild, hunters might shoot me,
But if I were wild, food might poison me,
But if I were wild, water might drown me.

Then he stops thinking

And . . .

The tiger behind the bars of his cage growls,
The tiger behind the bars of his cage snarls,
The tiger behind the bars of his cage roars.

Peter Niblett

160 Guidance

I want to get out,
I want to stay here,
I want to be welcomed,
I want to keep clear;
I want to believe,
I want to be sure.
Show me the man who knows the way, the truth, the life,
and who is yesterday, to-day and everlastingly the same;
tell me his name.

David S. Goodall

161   Out in the Fields with God

The little cares that fretted me,
       I lost them yesterday,
Among the fields above the sea,
       Among the winds at play,
Among the lowing of the herds,
       The rustling of the trees,
Among the singing of the birds,
       The humming of the bees.

The foolish fears of what might pass
       I cast them all away
Among the clover-scented grass
       Among the new-mown hay,
Among the hushing of the corn
       Where drowsy poppies nod,
Where ill thoughts die and good are born—
       Out in the fields with God.

Anon

162   Over the Hills and Far Away

Hark! how the drums beat up again,
For all true soldiers, gentlemen,
Then let us 'list and march, I say,
Over the hills and far away.

       O'er the hills and o'er the main
       To Flanders, Portugal and Spain.
       Queen Anne commands, and we'll obey,
       Over the hills and far away.

All gentlemen that have a mind
To serve the Queen that's good and kind,
Come 'list and enter into pay
Then over the hills and far away.

       O'er the hills and o'er the main *etc.*

Here's forty shillings on the drum
For those that volunteers to come,
With shirts, and clothes and present pay
When over the hills and far away.

O'er the hills and o'er the main *etc.*

No more from sound of drum retreat,
While Marlborough and Galloway beat
The French and Spaniards every day
When over the hills and far away.

O'er the hills and o'er the main *etc.*

He that is forced to go and fight
Will never get true honour by't,
While volunteers will win the day
When over the hills and far away.

O'er the hills and o'er the main *etc.*

Come then, boys, and you shall see
We every one shall captains be,
To dress and strut as well as they
When over the hills and far away.

O'er the hills and o'er the main *etc.*

For if we go 'tis one to ten
But we'll return as gentlemen,
All gentleman as well as they
When over the hills and far away.

O'er the hills and o'er the main *etc.*

What though our friends our absence mourn,
We with all honour shall return,
And then we'll sing both night and day
Over the hills and far away.

O'er the hills and o'er the main *etc.*

Traditional

163 Soldier, Soldier

'Soldier, soldier, won't you marry me,
  With your musket, fife and drum?'
'Oh no, sweet maid, I cannot marry you,
  For I have no hat to put on.'

So up she went to her grandfather's chest,
And she got him a hat of the very, very best,
  And the soldier put it on!

'Soldier, soldier, won't you marry me,
  With your musket, fife and drum?'
'Oh no, sweet maid, I cannot marry you,
  For I have no coat to put on.'

So up she went to her grandfather's chest,
And she got him a coat of the very, very best,
  And the soldier put it on!

'Soldier, soldier, won't you marry me,
  With your musket, fife and drum?'
'Oh no, sweet maid, I cannot marry you,
  For I have no boots to put on.'

So up she went to her grandfather's chest,
And she got him a pair of the very, very best,
  And the soldier put them on!

'Soldier, soldier, won't you marry me,
  With your musket, fife and drum?'
'Oh no, sweet maid, I cannot marry you,
  For I have a wife of my own!'

Traditional

164 A Prayer

Lord Jesus
I give you my hands
to do your work.
I give you my feet
to go your way.
I give you my eyes
to see as you do.
I give you my tongue
to speak your words.
I give you my mind
that you may think in me.
Above all, I give you my heart
that you may love in me your Father
and all mankind.
I give you my whole self
that you may grow in me,
so that it is you, Lord Jesus,
who live and work and pray in me.

Anon

165 Little

I am the sister of him
And he is my brother.
He is too little for us
To talk to each other.

So every morning I show him
My doll and my book;
But every morning he still is
Too little to look.

Dorothy Aldis

166 A Deserted Beach

Silently the little Crab crawled along the beach,
> The wind howls,
> The Crab rolls over,
> He hits a rock,
> The Crab lies still,
> There is no movement . . .
> He is dead.
> The beach is deserted, empty.

Where are the Sea-gulls and Oysters?
Where are the Cockles and Mussels?
Where are the Sandcastles?

They have been there,
But now . . . they have gone,
Where have they gone?
Nobody knows . . .
Except the greedy sea.

Robin Smallman

167 Questions

I often wonder why, oh why,
All grown-ups say to me:
'When you are old and six foot high,
What do you want to be?'

I sometimes wonder what they'd say
If I should ask them all
What they would like to be, if they
Were six years old and small.

Raymond Wilson

168   Death of a Cat

I rose early
On the fourth day
Of his illness,
And went downstairs
To see if he was
All right.

He was not in the
House, and I rushed
Wildly round the
Garden calling his name.

I found him lying
Under a rhododendron
Bush,
His black fur
Wet, and matted
With the dew.

I knelt down beside him.
And he opened his
Mouth as if to
Miaow
But no sound came.

I picked him up
And he lay quietly
In my arms
As I carried him
Indoors.

Suddenly he gave
A quiet miaow
And I felt his body tense,
And then lie still.

I laid his warm,
Lifeless body on
The floor, and
Rubbed my fingers
Through his fur.

A warm tear
Dribbled down
My cheek and
Left a salt taste
On my lips.

I stood up, and
Walked quietly
Out of the room.

Anthony Thompson

169   Funeral Blues

Stop all the clocks, cut off the telephone,
Prevent the dog from barking with a juicy bone,
Silence the pianos and with muffled drum
Bring out the coffin, let the mourners come.

Let aeroplanes circle moaning overhead
Scribbling on the sky the message He Is Dead,
Put crepe bows round the white necks of the public doves,
Let the traffic policeman wear black cotton gloves.

He was my North, my South, my East and West,
My working week and my Sunday rest,
My noon, my midnight, my talk, my song;
I thought that love would last for ever: I was wrong.

The stars are not wanted now; put out every one:
Pack up the moon and dismantle the sun;
Pour away the ocean and sweep up the wood:
For nothing now can ever come to any good.

W. H. Auden

170   I Went Back

I went back after a cold
And nothing was the same
When the register was called
Even my name
Sounded queer . . . new . . .
(And I was born here too!)
Everyone knew more than me,
Even Kenneth Hannacky
Who's worst usually.
They'd made a play
And puppets from clay
While I was away,
Learnt a song about Cape Horn,
Five guinea pigs were born.
Daffodils in the blue pot
(I planted them)
Bloomed and I was not there to see.
Jean had a new coat
And someone, probably George,
Smashed my paper boat.
Monday was a dreadful day
I wished I was still away.
Tuesday's news day.
I took my stamps to show,
Made a clown called John . . .
Cold's almost gone . . .
And . . . the smallest guinea pig,
Silky black and brown thing
I'm having till Spring.

Gwenn Dunn

171

Love thy neighbour as thyself.

Christianity

116

172 Waking Up

First the sound of sweeping through the
Small chink in the window; early sun
Knifing through the trees, and the sound
Of cars. The deep, vibrating noise of
Aircraft engines at Safdar Jung
Interminably beating across the silence of
Early morning, then quiet.
The feeling of freedom from an
English world of school, the feeling
Of waking slowly absorbing all the
Sounds that reawaken forgotten echoes
From a dim past, the longing
For endless freedom, endless bliss
In contemplating the day to come,
Without apprehension. Again
The sound of sweeping, and the
Raucous cawing of a bird.

R. R. Crook

173 Beginnings

At three o'clock in the morning if you
       open your window and listen
You will hear the feet of the wind that
       is going to call the sun,
And the trees in the darkness rustle,
And the trees in the moonlight glisten,
And though it is deep dark night, you
       know that the night is done.

Anon

174 The Story of Bonnie and Clyde

You've heard the story of Jesse James—
Of how he lived and died.
If you're still in need
Of something to read,
Here's the story of Bonnie and Clyde.

Now Bonnie and Clyde are the Barrow Gang.
I'm sure you all have read
How they rob and steal
And those who squeal
Are usually found dying or dead.

They call them cold hearted killers;
They say they're heartless and mean;
But I say this with pride,
That I once knew Clyde
When he was honest and upright and clean.

But the law's fooled around,
Kept taking him down
And locking him up in a cell,
Till he said to me,
I'll never be free,
So I'll meet a few of them in hell!

The road was so dimly lighted;
There were no highway signs to guide;
But they made up their minds,
If all roads were blind,
They wouldn't give up till they died.

The road gets dimmer and dimmer;
Sometimes you can hardly see;
But it's fight man to man,
And do all you can,
For they know they can never be free.

If they try to act like citizens,
And rent them a nice little flat,
About the third night
They're invited to fight,
By a sub-machine gun rat-tat-tat.

They don't think they are too tough or desperate,
They know the law always wins,
They have been shot at before
But they do not ignore
That death is the wages of sin.

From heartbreaks some people have suffered,
From weariness some people have died,
But take it all in all,
Our troubles are small,
Till we get like Bonnie and Clyde.

Some day they will go down together,
And they will bury them side by side.
To a few it means grief,
To the law it's relief,
But it's death to Bonnie and Clyde.

Bonnie Parker

175   Fidele

Fear no more the heat o' the sun,
Nor the furious winter's rages;
Thou thy worldly task hast done,
Home art gone, and ta'en thy wages;
Golden lads and girls all must,
As chimney-sweepers, come to dust.

From Cymbeline *William Shakespeare.*

176　Sing a Song of People

Sing a song of people
　　　　　Walking fast or slow;
People in the city,
　　　　　Up and down they go.

People on the sidewalk,
People on the bus;
People passing, passing,
In back and front of us.
People on the subway
Underneath the ground;
People riding taxis
Round and round and round.

People with their hats on,
Going in the doors;
People with umbrellas
When it rains and pours.
People in tall buildings
And in stores below;
Riding elevators
Up and down they go.

People walking singly,
People in a crowd;
People saying nothing,
People talking loud.
People laughing, smiling,
Grumpy people too;
People who just hurry
And never look at you!

Sing a song of people
　　　　　Who like to come and go;
Sing of city people
　　　　　You see but never know!

Lois Lenski

120

177 Dazzling New and Super You

The dazzling, new and super you,
So the adverts say,
It's there for sure at every store
Buy it now today.
Whenever you're lonely, bored or blue,
They claim to be selling dreams come true,
They tell you to buy and don't ask why
So the adverts say.

The gateway to glamour opens wide,
So the adverts say,
So bring your cash and step inside,
Now without delay.
It's never just toothpaste, scent or soap,
But a symbol of every thrill and hope,
And nothing need be outside its scope,
So the adverts say.

It's your money they're after, though that's not
What the adverts say,
And you and your dreams can go to pot
Once they've had their way.
So God of all wisdom, give us sense
When propaganda is most intense
Not to be so naïve as to believe
All the adverts say.

Roy Lawrence

178 Love

I love you,
Not only for what you are,
But for what I am
When I am with you.

Anon

179 Washing Day

The old woman must stand
At the tub, tub, tub,
The dirty clothes
To rub, rub, rub;
But when they are clean
And fit to be seen,
She'll dress like a lady
And dance on the green.

Anon

180 I Wish I Were

I wish I were a humbug
In a little boy's pocket;
And I wish I were a lamp bulb
In a lamp socket.

I wish I were a dustbin,
Full of odds and ends;
And I wish I were a puppy dog
With lots and lots of friends.

I wish I were an old boot
To be thrown at noisy cats;
I wish I were the West wind,
And could knock off people's hats.

I wish I were a Chinese book
Written in Peking,
And I wish I were a bunch of keys
Hanging on a ring.

I wish I were a mirror,
Hanging on a wall;
I wish I were so many things.
I cannot be them all.

D. Chisnall

181 My Father's Hands

My father's hands
are beautiful, they can
fix this moth's wing and make
machines
they can mend the fuse when the world
goes dark
can make the light swim and walls jump
in around me again
I can see my mother's face again.

You must take good care of them with
your finest creams
never let the nails break or
skin go dry, only those wise fingers
know how to fix the thing
that makes my doll cry and they make
small animals out of clay.

Never let blades or anything sharp
and hurtful near them
don't let bees or nettles
sting them don't let fire or burning oil
try them.

My father's hands are beautiful, take
good care of them.

Jeni Couzyn

182 There Is Always Someone

I had no shoes
         and complained,
           until I met a man
who had no feet.

An Arabian saying from Practical Christianity

183   People Like People

People like people who are kind
Kind to their mothers, kind to their fathers,
               kind to their family.
But do they like people who are kind to an enemy?
People like people like themselves

               And this means that anyone
               Who wants to be someone
               Must be like everyone else.

People like people in luck,
Lucky in love, lucky in work,
               lucky in every way.
But do they like people who are luckier than they?
People like people like themselves

               And this means that anyone *etc.*

People like people in love
Loving a husband, loving your wife,
               loving your parents,
But do they like people whose loving is different?
People like people like themselves

               And this means that anyone *etc.*

People like people who are good
Good to their neighbours, good to their friends,
               good to their parents.
But do they like people who are better than others?
People like people like themselves

               And this means that anyone *etc.*

Jeanette Stanley

184 Violence

Violence is something which comes out quickly
       Like rapids in a river—
It comes out unexpectedly
       and makes terror and harm.
It comes out fiercely
       and does not care what sorrow it makes.
It dirties the clean.
It makes people change.
It hardens the soft and
It kills the weak.

Gup Tippett (aged 13)

185   Famine

It was by chance that we were born
To plenty in a land of corn.

For some who were born
              In other lands
Less favoured by
              The weather's hand
It was a very bitter price
They paid for want of wheat and rice.

Nigeria's Northern deserts spread
And leave whole tribes to wait for death.

In Bangladesh the rains spill forth
And flood the plains from South to North.
They isolate the village folk
Who least can bear this heavy yolk.

It was sheer chance where we were born.
Should we not send them of our corn?

Christopher Daniels (aged 12)

186   The Creak

Creak!
Eerk!
I went down,
And a door opened.
I went in
And all it was,
Was the song of bird
Filling a bare room.

Paul White (aged 7)

187 Hidden Treasure

They told me there was treasure in my garden,
      If I'd only take a spade and dig,
And there wasn't much to measure in my garden,
      For it wasn't very big.

So I gave some of my leisure to my garden,
      And I dug it well from end to end;
But I didn't find the treasure in my garden—
      Or none that I could spend!

Yet I got a lot of pleasure from my garden,
      When the flowers grew thick and tall;
So perhaps that was the treasure in my garden
      After all!

T. Mark

188 A Nail

For want of a nail the shoe was lost,
For want of a shoe the horse was lost,
For want of a horse the rider was lost,
For want of a rider the battle was lost,
For want of a battle the kingdom was lost,
And all for the want of a horseshoe nail.

Anon

189 Happiness?

I feel a bit happier
When I see a kingfisher
In the spring green willows,
And the oak leaved ferns
By the lemon wood trees.

Clifton Roderick Foster (aged 11)

190 Cruelty

Tom tied a kettle to the tail of a cat,
Jill put a stone in the blind man's hat
Bob threw his grandmother down the stairs—
And they all grew up ugly, and nobody cares.

Anon

191 Always Finish

If a task is once begun,
Never leave it till it's done.
Be the labour great or small,
Do it well or not at all.

Anon

Prose

192

The other morning I was down at the orthopaedic workshop in the old dispensary buildings of the Queen Elizabeth II Hospital. It is a busy scene. Churchill Mohatlane, the young man in charge, has had special training in the making of artificial limbs. He is assisted by two paraplegics in wheel chairs and Francis, a deaf mute. I watched Boniface fitting sheepskin padding to a pair of crutches, while Churchill measured a young girl for calipers. Motlatsi was working on an artificial leg. In a chair, waiting, sat a tall strapping lass with bright dark eyes. She spoke good English and told me she was anxious to get back to her mountain school in time to write her last exam paper the next day.

She had come down to Maseru because her artificial leg had broken some time ago and was replaced by another so cumbersome that she walked with great difficulty. Churchill said he had hoped to adapt a leg recently given to Save the Children for this girl. He confirmed that the one she was using was a period piece, far too heavy and complicated to fit. But a new leg would cost R300 (£165 approx.).

From a letter written from Lesotho by Mary Manley and quoted in The World's Children, *December 1973*

193

This Special Exhibition is held on the 150th Anniversary of The Royal National Life-boat Institution 1824–1974.

The Royal National Life-boat Institution exists for the sole purpose of saving life at sea irrespective of race, colour or creed.

It provides, on call, the permanent day and night life-boat service necessary to cover known and predicted Search and Rescue requirements out to thirty miles from the coasts of the United Kingdom and the Republic of Ireland.

The British Isles comprise over 5000 separate islands and islets
Together, these account for something like 7000 miles of
coastline which is often dangerous because of frequent gales,
strong tides and shifting sandbanks. Fog is common in summer
as well as in winter, causing strandings and collisions.

It is, therefore, not surprising that the R.N.L.I. is the oldest
national life-boat service in the world. Since it was founded in
1824 it has saved nearly 100 000 lives.

From a poster issued by the Royal National Life-boat Institution

194   Your Country Needs You

Your country needs you! That's what they said, but they knew
they wouldn't come back, they'd be dead.

'Don't worry lads', he said, 'You'll be all right.' But how did he
know? He didn't have to fight. They said goodbye and went
away. They went to a trench and left friends and relatives
crying.

'Fifty thousand were killed today.' That's all he said. He didn't
care, he only planned the war, didn't fight, didn't help.

When the news came that we'd won, 'We won!' he cried. He
cared about 'our' victory.

*Written by Alison, aged 11, after some project work on World War I, which
included listening to* Oh What A Lovely War

195

Goodbye: To Mrs Kent after twenty five years service for the
school.
Welcome: to Mr Baker, our new caretaker.
Congratulations: *a* to Mrs De Martino on the birth of her
                daughter Sara
                b to Mrs Thomas (formerly Miss Cullum) on
                her marriage in April.

Thank you: *a* to Mr de Roux and Mrs Lewis who have joined
the staff,

b to Mrs Borkovic and the ladies of our new
kitchen. Long may their current efforts be
maintained.

From a junior school magazine

196   The Fire Station

Class Two visited the fire station, looked around very carefully
and got the answers to lots of questions. They found that the
station had been there for eleven years, there were twenty men
with five on each shift. Five men work on each appliance and
they can leave the station within fifteen seconds of getting an
alarm.

This year seventy three fires were dealt with, but one alarm in
ten is false. This year's most dangerous job was when a train
ran into a fire engine.

Fire drills are held every day and you must be eighteen before
you can become a fireman. There is a twelve week training
course in London. Each fireman has protective clothing and he
works two days, two nights and then two days off. There are
no emergency poles in Cheshunt station.

The last question was: 'How would you deal with a fire at the
top of the tower block of flats?'

Answer: 'There is a hydrant on each floor and the hoses are
worked from there'.

*Compiled by a class of second year junior school children after a visit to the local
fire station*

197   The Dustbin Men

The roaring of the dust-cart coming up the road. All the men
are jumping out. Their beards are full of dust and they have
faded blue shirts and hardened faces. His face in the air, one of
them whistles. Then his tough hands grip the dustbin and pull
it up onto his back. Now he shows strain. The dustbin is
heavy. He walks with a bent back and dragging feet. Then with
a sigh of relief he thrusts the old bottles, tin cans, paper bags
and all the rubbish into the dust-cart.

Kim (aged 10)

198

Dear Editors,
              I am very disappointed at all the birds' eggs being
stolen out of their nests by boys. Especially when they are
warm and going to have a baby. I also object to boys throwing
stones at birds and hurting them very badly or even killing
them. I think people should be fined for this and made, by
RSPB, to care for the bird and help it get better.

A bird lover

From the pages of a junior school magazine

199   The Cheetah

The cheetah is a savage, ruthless animal. His eyes are like
diamonds and his white sharp teeth are like stalactites hanging
from a cave. His fur is as soft as a feather and his claws as sharp
as piercing needles. He stretches in the blazing sun and sleeps.
His eyes closed he lies there for hours. His head is on one side
and he has an enchanted spell over him. He lies like a kitten by
the fire.

But who knows what he will do when he wakes up?

Debra (aged 11)

200 The Policemen Visit

On the 11 February two policemen came to visit us. Their names were Sergeant Ryecroft and Police Constable Hattrick. They said that there are 25 000 policemen in the Metropolitan Police.

The most popular police dog is the Alsatian.

The policemen said that they had one policewoman at their station. They said we must never accept lifts from people we don't know, not even if they say they are a friend of our mother or father. They also said that we must never accept sweets from people we don't know.

They said that Cheshunt didn't have any police horses, and that England was the only country where policemen went on their beat unarmed.

Policemen travel by Panda car, helicopter, motor cycle, bicycle, river boat and van. The police force sometimes has dogs and horses at their stations. The dogs are for tracking down people and the horses are for policemen to ride in crowds and the country.

The policemen told us that Cheshunt police station had one police dog. They also told us the name of the old police dog. It was Quinton. The old police dog got old and died so Cheshunt police station got another dog.

We can tell a Sergeant from a Police Constable because a Sergeant has got three V shapes on his arms.

The policeman carries a truncheon, keys, whistle, handcuffs, notebook and torch. He carries the truncheon in a pocket down his right leg. The policeman wears a blue jacket and trousers and a helmet or flat cap.

Debbie (aged 10)

201 'Thousands Will Die'–Drought Warning

Hundreds of thousands of people will die in the drought-ravaged Sahel region of West Africa unless international aid operations are speeded up, Mr William Price, Parliamentary Secretary at the Ministry of Overseas Development, said yesterday.

He was speaking on his return to London after a nine day tour of Chad, Volta and Mali.

'There has been too much talking and too little action,' he said. 'The whole operation is running well behind schedule. The food should have been in the region before the June rains and it is clear that much of it will not arrive.'

It was a desperate race against time to get food to the countries to distribute it inland, and to get starving nomadic people into the refugee camps.

'We saw people arriving in a refugee camp without their mat tents. They had eaten them on the way.'

The government and charitable organisations are sending sixty lorries to the region. Mr Price will give a detailed report to Mrs Hart, Minister of Overseas Development, before she visits Brussels to discuss aid schemes with Common Market ministers

By the Diplomatic Correspondent Daily Telegraph *27 April 1974*

202 Where We Live (1)

Our little village was a happy, comfortable place to live in, although it wasn't very beautiful; there were too many mills with their tall chimneys pouring out black smoke and soot. We now had an Electric Tramcar to take us into Oldham if we wanted anything special. This was a treat for George and me, and if Grandma wanted something really special, we all went by Tramcar to Manchester, which was a Great Day. We had tea in a cafe called Smallman's, with waitresses in black, with stiff white aprons, who brought us lots of cakes with icing on.

Although they brought us so many, we could only choose one each, in case we got upset, as we had a long journey back on the Tram. Although Manchester was very large, and had such wonderful things to see, it was very tiring, and George and I had great difficulty keeping awake on our journey home. When we went on a special outing to the Big Shops, we left our two dogs, Gyp and Barney, at home, because Mother was afraid they might get their paws trodden on in the crowds. They were very glad to see us when we got home.

From Miss Carter Came With Us *By Helen Bradley*

203 Where We Live (2)

'Get yourself off home!' shouted the men when they saw Miss Smith and her little band of suffragettes, who had marched out on a cold January day. It was rather frightening. One man shook Miss Carter (who wore Pink) and she fainted in the middle of the road. Father came home with the news that some dreadful women had been walking through the streets shouting 'Votes for Women'. 'Fancy women wanting the vote—never heard of such tomfoolery,' he said. 'Jane, I hope that neither you nor your sisters have anything to do with it.'

Mother said, 'No, Frederick, of course not,' but she looked at George and me with a twinkle in her eye.

From Miss Carter Came With Us *by Helen Bradley*

204 A Child's View of War

I understand what war is. I was very sad because we slept in shelters and I could not go out into the sunshine. I could not forget the terrible thoughts I had. When I fell asleep at night, I cried. And I cried again in my sleep because I dreamed about the war.

In the morning when I awoke, I looked out of the shelter, but I could see no cat, no dog. I realised that they were as afraid as I was. That is how I first understood the meaning of war.

When I was young I did not know what war meant.

Written by an eight year old Israeli child who had been involved in fighting between Israelis and Arabs at Qiryat Shemona, where eighteen people, including eight children, were killed by Arab marauders.

Daily Telegraph *26 April 1974*

205 Mad Lucas

April 1974 was the hundredth anniversary of the death of one of the strangest characters ever to live in Hertfordshire.

James Lucas was thirty six when his mother died but he was so devoted to her that after her death he became a hermit. With only two cats for company he began to live a strange life in his house near Great Wymondly.

He gave up washing, changing his clothes, or making any attempt to keep the house clean. Soon he and his house were so filthy that people came from miles around to look at both him and his house, as if they were some fairground sideshow.

Lucas enjoyed this and amongst the thousands of people who went to stare at him was Charles Dickens. Despite being such an extraordinary man Mad Lucas was always kind to tramps, people with no homes, and especially children.

Children seemed to accept him instinctively as a friendly man. They were not frightened by his hairy, unkempt and filthy appearance and he gave very generously to local children.

As he got older he employed two guards to protect him from sightseers who got too inquisitive, and other intruders. He wouldn't let the guards live in the house with him, and they stayed in huts in the garden.

On April 17 1874 the guards found Mad Lucas unconscious and he died two days later. He had one more sensation to offer the world. When the appalling filth and squalor of his house was being searched and cleaned up, sums of money totalling £20 000 were found.

Elissa Milsome

206

'Here they come! Here they come!' Gunlocks clicked.

Across the smoke-infested fields came a brown swarm of running men who were giving shrill yells. They came on, stooping and swinging their rifles at all angles. A flag tilted forward, sped near the front.

As he caught sight of them, the youth was momentarily startled by a thought that perhaps his gun was not loaded. He stood trying to rally his faltering intellect so that he might recollect the moment when he had loaded but he could not.

A hatless general pulled his dripping horse to a stand near the colonel of the 304th. He shook his fist in the other's face. 'You've got to hold 'em back!' he shouted savagely; 'you've got to hold 'em back!'

In his agitation the colonel began to stammer. 'A-ll r-right, general, all right, by Gawd! We-we'll do our-we-we'll d-d-do-do our best, general.' The general made a passionate gesture and galloped away. The colonel, perchance to relieve his feelings, began to scold like a wet parrot. The youth turning swiftly to make sure that the rear was unmolested, saw the commander regarding his men in a highly resentful manner, as if he regretted above everything his association with them.

The man at the youth's elbow was mumbling, as if to himself, 'Oh, we're in for it now! Oh, we're in for it now!'

The captain of the company had been pacing excitedly to and fro in the rear. He coaxed in school-mistress fashion, as to a congregation of boys with primers. His talk was an endless repetition. 'Reserve your fire boys—don't shoot till I tell you—save your fire—wait till they get close up—don't be damned fools—'

Perspiration streamed down the youth's face, which was soiled like that of a weeping urchin. He frequently, with a nervous movement, wiped his eyes with his coat-sleeve. His mouth was still a little ways open. . .

. . . 'Well, we've helt 'em back. We've helt 'em back; derned if we haven't.' The men said it blissfully, leering at each other with dirty smiles.

The youth turned to look behind him and off to the right and off to the left. He experienced the joy of a man who at last finds leisure in which to look about him.

Underfoot there were a few ghastly forms motionless. They lay twisted in fantastic contortions. Arms were bent and heads were turned in incredible ways. It seemed that the dead men must have fallen from some great height to get into such positions. They looked to be dumped out upon the ground from the sky.

From The Red Badge of Courage *by Stephen Crane*

207   The Rabbit

When we were children our father often worked on the night shift. Once it was spring time, and he used to arrive home, black and tired, just as we were downstairs in our nightdresses

Then night met morning face to face, and the contact was not always happy. Perhaps it was painful to my father to see us gaily entering upon the day into which he dragged himself soiled and weary. He didn't like going to bed in the spring morning sunshine.

But sometimes he was happy, because of his long walk through the dewy fields in the first daybreak. He loved the open morning, the crystal and the space, after a night down the pit. He watched every bird, every stir in the trembling grass, answered the whinnying of the peewits and tweeted to the wrens. If he could, he also would have whinnied and tweeted and whistled in a native language that was not human. He liked non-human things best.

One sunny morning we were all sitting at table when we heard his heavy slurring walk up the entry. We became uneasy. His was always a disturbing presence, trammelling. He passed the window darkly, and we heard him go into the scullery and put down his tin bottle. But directly he came into the kitchen we felt at once that he had something to communicate. No one spoke. We watched his black face for a second.

'Give me a drink,' he said.

My mother hastily poured out his tea. He went to pour it out into his saucer. But instead of drinking he suddenly put something on the table among the tea cups. A tiny brown rabbit! A small, small rabbit, a mere morsel, sitting against the bread as still as if it were a made thing.

'A rabbit! A young one! Who gave it to you, father?'

But he laughed enigmatically, with a sliding motion of his yellow, grey eyes, and went to take off his coat. We pounced on the rabbit.

'Is it alive? Can you feel its heartbeat?'

My father came back and sat down heavily in his armchair. He dragged his saucer to him and blew his tea, pushing out his red lips under his black moustache.

'Where did you get it from father?'

'I picked it up.' . . .

. . . On the field path my father had found a dead mother rabbit and three little dead ones—this one alive, but unmoving.

From Phoenix *by D. H. Lawrence*

208   Don't Say It

I hope you never say 'Drop dead!' to anybody. You can't know what it's like for somebody you love to die. My mother died when she was swept away in a flood.

I felt desperate, full of despair and loneliness. It was as if there was never any sun in the day, or any moon at night. For a long time I didn't believe that such a thing could happen to me. I didn't ever want to believe it.

So don't ever say things like 'Drop dead!' to anybody. You'll never know what it's like to lose somebody you love—until you do.

Schoolgirl (aged 13)

209   Protest

The response to the call for satyagraha* was vast beyond all expectations. . . The authorities responded with violence. Police beat demonstrators with steel tipped staves, and in Delhi fired on them. In Punjab where unrest had been active even before the satyagraha, mob violence broke out, and Gandhi, setting off from Bombay in the hope of calming the situation, was turned back by the British. There were outbreaks of violence in other parts of the country, and then, on 13 April,

* 'Satyagraha' is the Indian word meaning 'truth force', which was a non-violent passive protest by Indians who were seeking independence for their country.

142

the most shocking event since the Mutiny, when Brigadier General Dyer in Amritsar ordered his Gurkhas and Baluchis to fire into the crowd assembled for a demonstration in the Jallianwala Bagh: 379 people were killed and more than a thousand were wounded.

From Gandhi *by George Woodcock*

210 Police Leave Cancelled to Meet Soccer Fans

All police leave has been cancelled in Stoke-on-Trent for tonight's football match between Stoke City and Manchester United. The move is to prevent any repetition of Saturday's invasion by United fans of the Old Trafford pitch.

At Manchester more than thirty supporters were arrested and around two hundred escorted from the ground after numerous running battles. The game against Manchester City was abandoned after eighty five minutes. . .

Wounding and assault.

The weekend soccer hooliganism also struck Blackpool where Middlesbrough fans celebrated promotion to the First Division after beating Preston North End.

Some twenty fans are to appear in court today charged with a number of offences, including wounding, assault on police and theft.

The trouble began after some of the coach firms advertised a night out in Blackpool as an added attraction following the match at Preston.

'The coaches did not leave the resort until late on Saturday night and as a result groups of youngsters were roaming about with nothing to do,' said Superintendent Alan Rydsheard, head of Blackpool police.

Daily Telegraph *29 April 1974*

143

211 'I need help . . . No-one wants me. No-one cares.'

A lonely old widow was found dying. Ethel left a diary of despair—terrifying loneliness was the real cause of her death. Yet she lived in a bustling factory town.

It should never have happened. Yet there are thousands of lonely, despairing old people like Ethel.

Help the Aged works to bring needy old people the happiness that should be their heritage. It provides flats designed for their needs where they find friendship and a thoughtful warden on hand; and Day Centres where they can meet, find interest and low-cost meals. Much more needs to be done.

Every £2 you give to provide flats is multiplied twenty-fold thanks to loans. £25 provides £500 worth of housing. £150 names a flat in memory of someone dear to you. £250 names a double flat.

Every lonely day is a torment to those in need. Please send quickly to:

The Hon. Treasurer,
The Rt. Hon Lord Maybray-King,
Help the Aged, Room A1,
8, Denman Street, London W1A 2AP.

212 Persuasion—True or False?

RIGHT NOW, YOU'LL BE MORE COMFORTABLY OFF IN A VICTOR.

More comfortably off, because the Victor is all space and light and luxury.

And more comfortably off, because a Victor is remarkably easy on your pocket, both to run and to buy. And that goes for both the Victor 1800 and 2300, saloon or estate.

144

THE RIGHT ECONOMY, RIGHT NOW.

The price starts as low as £1414 plus VAT for the Victor 1800 saloon. And it tours at 29.3 miles per gallon according to *What Car*. Even the powerful 2300 model is a petrol miser. *The Guardian* found its average touring consumption is 28 miles per gallon. But there's more to the Victor than petrol economy.

THE RIGHT COMFORT, RIGHT NOW.

The Victor actually has more usable space inside than many cars that cost a lot more.

There's 42.1 inches of leg room and 55.4 inches of shoulder room in the front, just a little less in the back.

The boot takes 21 cubic feet of luggage, and if you want more, the Victor Estate gives it to you.

From a Vauxhall advertisement

213

For nothing is greater or better than this when man and wife dwell in the house in harmony: a grief to their foes and a joy to their friends. But this they know best themselves.

Homer Odyssey *VI 182–185*

214

By the time he is fourteen the average American child has seen 18 000 deaths on television.

215

. . . Turning towards the hearth, where the two logs had fallen apart, and sent forth only a red uncertain glimmer, he seated himself on his fireside chair, and was stooping to push his logs together, when to his blurred vision it seemed as if there were gold on the floor in front of the hearth. Gold—his own gold—brought back to him as mysteriously as it had been taken away! He felt his heart begin to beat violently, and for a few moments he was unable to stretch out his hand and grasp the restored treasure. The heap of gold seemed to glow and get larger beneath his agitated gaze. He leaned forward at last, and stretched forth his hand; but instead of the hard coin with the familiar resisting outline, his fingers encountered soft warm curls. In utter amazement Silas fell on his knees and bent his head low to examine the marvel; it was a sleeping child—a round, fair thing, with soft yellow rings all over its head. Could this be his little sister come back to him in a dream—his little sister whom he had carried about in his arms for a year before she died, when he was a small boy without shoes or stockings? That was the first thought that darted across Silas's blank wonderment. Was it a dream? He rose to his feet again, pushed his logs together, and, throwing on some dried leaves and sticks, raised a flame. But the flame did not disperse the vision; it only lit up more distinctly the little round form of the child, and its shabby clothing. It was very much like his little sister. Silas sank into his chair powerless, under the double presence of an inexplicable surprise and a hurrying influx of memories. How and when had the child come in without his knowledge?

From Silas Marner *by George Eliot*

216 Eyam

Eyam is also famous for an event which took place 300 years ago and which has stirred the hearts of men ever since. This was the visitation of the village by the Great Plague from London at the end of August 1665. The story unfolds of how a parcel of cloth was brought by carrier from London, and set down at the door of the local tailor, a man call George Viccars, who lived at a cottage still standing just west of the Churchyard. Unfortunately, the cloth had become infected with the Plague germs before being despatched, and the tailor soon became the Plague's first victim in Eyam. At this stage it would have been easy for the remainder of the inhabitants to seek safety in flight. Had they done so, they might have been responsible for spreading the Plague over a large part of the North of England, and it is to their eternal glory that acting under the inspired leadership of two men, William Mompesson, rector of Eyam, and Thomas Stanley, who had been his immediate predecessor, but had become a Nonconformist on his refusal to subscribe to the Act of Uniformity, the inhabitants voluntarily cut themselves off from contact with the outside world, so that the pestilence should not be spread elsewhere. It meant death for many of them, for during the fifteen months that the Plague did its dread work, 260 persons perished out of a presumed total population of 350. In the fields in and around Eyam you can see mute memorials to that sad time in the form of tombstones erected over victims who were buried near the places where they died, e.g. the Riley Graves, where members of the Hancock family lie buried, and the Lydgate Graves, in the village.

From Eyam Parish Church, Notes for Visitors

217   Centenary Exhibition of Marconi

The Marchesa Marconi, widow of the wireless pioneer who died in 1937, last night opened his centenary exhibition— entitled 'I'll put a girdle round about the Earth'—at the Science Museum, London. It will remain open for six months from today.

Guglielmo Marconi was born in Italy 100 years ago today. The anniversary is being marked by the Institution of Electrical Engineers with a day of lectures called 'The Marconi Heritage' followed in the evening by a soirée.

The company archives have provided much of the material displayed in the exhibition. It includes machines used by Marconi as well as papers relating to his promise to 'put a girdle round about the Earth' quicker than the forty minutes required by Shakespeare's Puck.

After making his early experiments in the attic of his parents' villa near Bologna, in Italy, Marconi came to London in 1896, aged twenty two. He did most of his work in Britain, only returning to his native country because of ill-health two years before he died.

In 1899 he enabled two British warships to exchange messages though they were seventy five miles apart. Two years later came the most triumphant moment of his life, when three faint dots of a Morse signal transmitted from Cornwall were heard 2000 miles across the Atlantic in Newfoundland.

He shared a Nobel prize for physics in 1909 for his contribution to wireless telegraphy.

Daily Telegraph 1974

218   Help

At Heathrow Airport there is an organisation called the Travellers' Help Unit. It was established to help travellers in need, and last year (1973) it gave assistance to eleven hundred people.

The people who organised this unit speak many languages between them. The cases with which they deal include runaways, robbery victims, people who have been deported, others who are returning to England without relatives, friends or money, and many people who have personal problems.

From a diocesan news letter

219   The Right to Serve

Alec Dickson, who founded Voluntary Service Overseas in 195 and Community Service Volunteers four years later, can reflect on a considerable achievement as he celebrates his sixtieth birthday today.

In the space of sixteen years he has helped through these organisations no fewer than 28 000 Britons to give something of their lives to others. Thirteen thousand have spent at least a year abroad giving help.

Dickson first became involved in social work after Munich, when he left London to undertake refugee relief among Sudeten-German refugees in Czechoslovakia. He tells me one of the big changes in recent years has been in the selection of volunteers.

'In the days when I was getting VSO established we strove to choose the most outstanding, believing that it was a privilege to serve overseas. Today, in Community Service Volunteers, we are taking blind eighteen year-olds, young blacks and Borstal boys—in the belief that young people have a right to serve their country.'

Daily Telegraph *23 May 1974*

220

'What's the matter?' the girl asked.

Usually Sammy wouldn't have bothered to explain; not to a girl with her hair in short tufts, tied with blue ribbon and sticking out like horns. But he was tired. He needed someone. There was sympathy in her voice, a Red Cross look in her face, and he could use a bit of that, too.

'The pony,' Sammy said.

No fiction about a racehorse. No nonsense about shining like the front-room table. The truth was big enough.

'Hurt herself,' Sammy said. 'Down the orchard.'

The girl ran to the house. He thought she'd turned away, like the others, never listening. But she came back quickly, struggling into a coat and holding out a torch. He was surprised a girl could show such sense. He took the torch and ran, defying her to keep with him. She kept with him, her tufts bobbing, a hand pressed to her side in denial of the stitch. Not until they were going down the steepest incline did she almost stumble and throw out a hand. Against his principles Sammy took it, letting her cling as they sped past the general store and the telephone kiosk and the corner pub. They reached the gate and struggled over. They panted up the slope towards the brambles.

There Sammy stopped, his courage giving out. He didn't want to go around the barrier, to see what was on the other side. The girl looked at him, wondering what he was waiting for. He took a deep breath and stepped over the brambles, surprised by the darkness which the tree made. He couldn't see. He switched on the torch, screening it with his fingers because a sudden beam would frighten. The mare was standing. She was not alone.

Sammy flicked the light to what was on the ground. He made an incredulous sound and stepped closer. The mare's ears flattened, warning him to step carefully. All right, Sammy thought, I won't take it away nor frighten nor touch it even. He kept his fingers over the light and crouched until he was close enough to see clearly. Incredulity became relief and relief became a laugh which shook his stomach and pricked his eyes and tasted of tears in his throat.

'Is it all right?' the girl whispered.

All right? Sammy thought. It's blimmin' marvellous. 'Come and see,' he said.

The mare nudged the foal but it didn't understand. It pretended it couldn't rise. She coaxed and chided and persuaded and finally it stood, its long legs wavering, its face bewildered. She moved slightly, making discovery easier. It stood alongside her, its stump of tail in her face. She nudged it towards the secret place. The foal blundered and fumbled and almost found it. It tried again and succeeded. Its tail became articulate, throbbing with excitement.

150

For a while the mare thought only about the foal and its need for milk. Then she looked around to Sammy, asking for congratulations. Sammy gave them, as big as bouquets; you're the best, I always said you were the best, the bravest and wisest. The mare smiled, doubting she was as wonderful as that. Still, it was nice to be appreciated. She heaved a long sigh and gave in to her tiredness and dozed, eyes still open but bottom lip drooping, a hind hoof poised to show she was at peace.

'Hush,' Sammy hissed, although the girl had made no sound.

We got be be dead still, Sammy thought, never a sound, not breathing even. We got to be . . . Sammy almost said it, if only in his thoughts. He almost said reverent, we got to be reverent; except that reverence was a Sunday thing, dressed up in robes and special voices. His hand made a crouch-down motion and the girl crouched beside him while the rain seeped and the sounds of the city came from another world. They were fascinated by the first miracle, as old as life yet as new as now.

From The Love Affair *by Vian Smith*

221 Freedom

We've come to see the power of non-violence. We've come to see that this method is not a weak method, for it's the strong man who can stand up amid opposition, who can stand up against violence being inflicted upon him, and not retaliate with violence.

From a speech by Dr Martin Luther King in Detroit, 23 June 1963

222 Responsibility?

I swear by God this sacred oath, that I will render unconditional obedience to Adolf Hitler, the Fuhrer of the German Reich and people, Supreme Commander of the Armed

Forces, and will be ready as a brave soldier to risk my life at any time for this oath.

Oath of allegiance sworn by every member of the German army between 1934 and 1945

223   Trapped

The block of flats stood up like a giant box of cornflakes. It was nine storeys high and the top was flat. Above the top there was nothing but sky. Miles of empty blue.

The block was surrounded by lawns. They were like green carpets worn threadbare in parts where the boys played football. There was a car-park where a few old cars rested peacefully, and there was a playground square. This was tarmac with swings, a slide, a see-saw and an old oak tree.

The tree was massive, huge. It was old, and had been scarred with initials and carvings, and it was the only tree growing near the flats. Its roots were buried beneath tons of concrete.

A thick rope hung from one of its branches. Children swung on this rope when the caretaker was out. The caretaker was almost as old as the oak, and he could turn very nasty when he wished. For ages he'd threatened to cut the rope down.

From the ninth floor of the flats you could see the whole town spread out like a map. The houses looked like match-boxes, and traffic seemed to crawl along the roads like grumbling insects. Stevie stood on the balcony of his mother's ninth floor flat and he looked out on the world. The sky was clear. Just mile after mile of empty blue.

Stevie gazed down on the playground square. Like the sky it was empty. The swings squeaked in the wind. The thick rope dangled from its branch. The sun sparkled on the polished slide. It all seemed so dead. Even the giant oak looked dead. Stevie looked at the tree. It's trapped, he thought, trapped in the tarmac. It's like me, he thought, it's trapped like me.

As he stared a boy came on to the playground pulling a home-made go-kart. The boy sat down beside the oak tree. Stevie watched him then went back into the flat and drank the glass of milk that his mother had left for him. He went to the door and tried it. As usual it was locked.

He shrugged his shoulders and went back on to the balcony. High up in the blue sky an aeroplane was creeping past. It was so high up that Stevie could hardly see it. The boy on the go-kart was also looking for the aeroplane. He shaded his eyes against the sun and squinted. Stevie looked down at him. The boy waved lazily. Stevie wanted to wave back but he didn't. He remembered what his mother had said.

'You stay in, you hear,' she had told him. 'I'll be back for dinner, so you stay in. I'll lock the door. You hear me?' He had heard her. It was the usual thing. While she was in town Stevie had to stay in the flat. She didn't want him outside when she was away. She was afraid that Stevie would annoy the caretaker again. There had been lots of trouble when he'd set fire to one of the caretaker's dustbins.

'I'm trapped,' thought Stevie, 'I'm trapped like the old oak tree.'

Wes Magee Teachers' World *9 July 1971*

224 Charity Appeal

This year's main charity appeal was in aid of the Imperial Cancer Research Fund. Our target was to raise six hundred and seven pounds to buy a microscope to aid their important work in their laboratories. Our appeal was started by Mr McLeod, Appeals Secretary of the Fund, who visited us with a film to tell us of the research they conduct.

Then the inter-form competition began with each form competing to be awarded the cup for raising the most money. The school worked hard at such fund raising activities as sponsored walks and cycles, raffles, tuck shops and competitions. The winners were 1C with sixty eight pounds seventy eight and a half pence and 3W were runners-up with fifty eight pounds ninety three pence.

The sixth form also played a big part, and were responsible for raising a large proportion of the money. They organised a dance in aid of the charity (one hundred and thirty pounds) and a sponsored walk (two hundred and eleven pounds sixty three and a half pence). An individual prize was awarded to the person raising most money on his own. A sixth form boy, Michael Pinnock, was given this for raising thirty two pounds twenty five pence on the sponsored walk.

By the 17 May we had exceeded our target by raising six hundred and thirty five pounds twenty five pence, and Mr McLeod again visited us to be presented with our cheque and to award the cup and individual prize.

Janet Towers

225   Watching a Bird

Am I watching the bird or is he watching me? He looks very warily in my direction then moves and again he will stop to look at me. I think it is a blue tit. Its underneath is a very lovely yellowy-orange with a blue tail and its back is a greyish-blue. The neck is a rich velvety blackish-brown and the middle part of the head is white with a bar of brown across the eye and its cap is a very beautiful blue. Its wings are blue and yellow stripes.

In our garden we have a bird table which has fat hanging from a piece of wood. This is a favourite playground for tits. 'My bird' jumps up and clings to it. He looks very pretty hanging upside down on the bacon rinds, swinging this way and that and then trying to walk up the fat, slipping, again trying and succeeding. It pecks the fat there and then tries again, but he notices a flock of chattering starlings approaching. It cries 'Tsee, tsee, ch-ch-ch-ch-ch', and then flies away keeping at a safe distance. At last the starlings leave and he returns once again to his antics. He seems to be completely at home when he is hanging upside down. He is only four and a half inches long, perhaps that is why he is occasionally known as a tom tit after Tom Thumb who was very small. He's at it again. Up! Down! Up! Down! It makes me feel quite dizzy. Oh Dear! The starlings have returned. My blue tit has flown completely away.

Michael (aged 12)

226 A Morning Assembly

Gryce was straining over the top of the lecturn like a bulldog up on its hind legs.

'It's every morning alike! As soon as the hymn is announced you're off revving up! Hm-mmm! Hm-mmm! It's more like a race track in here than an assembly hall!' . . .

. . . No-one moved. Not a foot scraped. Not a page stirred. The teachers looked seriously into the ranks of the boys. The boys stood looking up at Gryce, each one convinced that Gryce was looking at him.

The silence thickened; the boys began to swallow their Adam's apples, their eyes skittering about in still heads. The teachers began to glance at each other and glance side-ways up at the platform.

Then a boy coughed.

'Who did that?'

Everybody looked round.

'I said WHO DID THAT?'

The teachers moved in closer, alert like a riot squad.

'Mr Crossley! Somewhere near you! Didn't you see the boy?'

'There, Crossley! That's where it came from! Around there!'

Crossley grabbed a boy by the arm and began to yank him into the open.

'It wasn't me, Sir!'

'Of course it was you.'

'It wasn't, Sir, honest!'

'Don't argue lad, I saw you.'

Gryce thrust his jaw over the front of the lectern, the air whistling down his nostrils.

'MACDOWALL! I might have known it! Get to my room lad!'

Crossley escorted Macdowall from the hall. Gryce waited for the doors to stop swinging, then replaced his stick and addressed the school.

'Right. We'll try again. Hymn one hundred and seventy five.'

The pianist struck the chord. Moderately slow it said in the book, but this direction was ignored by the school, and the tempo they produced was dead slow, the words delivered in a grinding monotone.

'New ev-ery morn-ing is the love
Our waken-ing and up-ris-ing prove;
Through sleep and dark-ness safe-ly brought,
Re-stored to life, and power, and thought.'

'STOP.'

The pianist stopped playing. The boys stopped singing.

'And what's that noise supposed to represent? I've heard sweeter sounds in a slaughter house! This is supposed to be a hymn of joy, not a dirge! So get your heads up, and your book up, and open your mouths and SING.'

There was a mass bracing of backs and showing of faces as Gryce stepped round the lectern to the edge of the platform and leaned out over the well of the hall.

'Or I'll make you sing like you've never sung before.'

From A Kestrel for a Knave *by Barry Hines*

156

He opened his mouth to speak but Carrie had turned. She said, 'Shut the door!' The woman looked puzzled—people were always so slow, Carrie thought. She said desperately, 'Miss Evans sent us for the goose. But something chased us. We ran and ran but it chased us. Sort of gobbling.'

The woman peered where she pointed, out into the night.

'Oh, shut the door,' Carrie cried. 'It'll come in.'

The woman smiled broadly. She had lovely, white teeth with a gap in the middle. 'Bless you, love, it's only Mister Johnny. I didn't know he was out.'

'He went to shut up the chickens,' Albert Sandwich said. 'Expect he went for a walk after.'

'But it wasn't a person,' Carrie said, speaking slowly to make them understand. She wasn't so frightened now. Albert had spoken so calmly that it made her calm too. She said, 'It didn't talk, it went gobble-gobble.'

'That's Mister Johnny's way of talking,' Albert Sandwich said. 'You must admit, Hepzibah, it could frighten someone.' He looked at Carrie, quite sternly. 'Though I expect you frightened him just as much. How would you feel if people ran away from you when you didn't mean to hurt them?'

Hepzibah called softly into the darkness, 'It's all right, Mister Johnny, all right, come in.' Her voice wasn't Welsh. A different, throatier, accent.

Someone appeared in the doorway and stood close to Hepzibah, as if for protection. A small person in a tweed suit and a spotted bow tie with a shy, scrumpled-up face. He tried to smile but he couldn't smile properly; one side of his mouth seemed dragged down.

Hepzibah said, 'This is Mister Johnny Gotobed, children. Mister Johnny, say how-do-you-do to our visitors, will you?'

He looked at her and made that queer sound in his throat. Chuckle-gobble—only now it did seem like talking. Some strange, unknown language. He rubbed his right hand on his trousers and looked at it. Then held it out, shakily.

Carrie couldn't move. Though he wasn't a ghost she was still too scared to touch that small, shaky hand. But Nick said, 'Hallo, Mister Johnny,' and went up to him as if it were the easiest and most natural thing in the world. 'I'm Nick,' he said. 'Nicholas Peter Willow and I'm just ten. It was my birthday last week. And Carrie, my sister, will be twelve next May.'

'Hch. Harch-a. Chala. Larschla,' Mister Johnny said. He spat a bit as he spoke and Carrie dreaded the moment when she would have to shake hands and be spat at.

But Hepzibah saved her. She said, 'The goose is ready for you. But you'll take a little something first, won't you? Albert, take Carrie to fetch the goose while I set the table.'

Albert took a candle from the dresser and lit it. Carrie followed him, through a door at the back of the kitchen, down a stone passage into a dairy. The goose lay, neatly trussed, on a cold, marble slab. There were speckly eggs in trays on the shelf, slabs of pale, oozy butter, and a big bowl of milk with a skin of cream on the top.

Carrie felt hollow with hunger. She said, 'I thought Mr Gotobed was dead. Mr Evan's sister's husband.'

'That's not him,' Albert said. 'Mister Johnny is a sort of distant cousin of that Mr Gotobed. He used to live in Norfolk but when his parents died he came here with Hepzibah. She's been his nurse since he was born.' He looked at Carrie as he set the candle down to give himself two free hands for the goose. 'Bit of a shock, I suppose, the first time.'

Holding the bag open so he could put the goose in, Carrie said, 'Is he mad?'

'No more than a lot of people. Just a bit simpler than some. Innocent, is what Hepzibah calls him.'

From Carrie's War *by Nina Bawden*

228

Tien Pao's hand jerked nervously in the lieutenant's grasp. Then with a loud, wild yell he jerked himself free, plunged down the revetment, plunged unseeing past the interpreter coming up with Glory-of-the-Republic, and tore madly across the crushed stone roadway straight at the roller. He plunged among the mass of tugging, chanting women. The roller stopped. There was an alarmed cackle of voices. The overseer barked loud, fierce words at the excited women, but the roller stood still. Tien Pao flung himself at a woman in the midst of the group. 'MY MOTHER!'

The overseer ranted and shrieked. It made no matter. The women stood twisted in the ropes, they huddled around a kneeling, weeping woman who sobbed herself out against her son's chest. The women wept with her, laughed, asked bewildered questions that no one heard and no one answered.

Then Leiutenant Hamsun was there. He yelled something fierce at the ranting Chinese overseer, and behind him the interpreter with the little pig stopped to explain things to the overseer to calm him down. But Lieutenant Hamsun elbowed his way in among the women, waded into the heap of kneeling women. Tien Pao's mother, her eyes streaming looked blindly up at him. 'The father! The father!' she chattered wildly. 'He is there on the mountain, he too must know it is Tien Pao.'

'I'll go get the jeep,' Lieutenant Hamsun shouted. Nobody heard him.

Tien Pao's mother wrenched herself out of the harness rope, grabbed Tien Pao's hand, and together they broke out of the heap of excited, chattering women. Tien Pao, not knowing what he was doing, pulled away from her, dashed to the interpreter, grabbed the little pig, and tore back to his mother. Together, hand in hand, they started running toward the distant, darkening mountain.

From far down the runway Lieutenant Hamsun shouted after them: 'The jeep, the jeep! What's the jeep for? You can't run all that way . . .'

They didn't hear him, and Lieutenant Hamsun turned and went on a limping run for the jeep. He forgot about the interpreter waiting near the roller, he forgot about roads and runways, he set out after Tien Pao and his mother across the rough field. He caught up with them. He almost had to lift Tien Pao's mother bodily into the jeep, she was too bewildered in her happy, delirious joy to be able to comprehend anything. The Lieutenant set out for the mountain. He couldn't reach it. The strewn jagged rocks and enormous boulders hurled below the mountainside by dynamite blasts forced him to stop far from the foot of the dug-away mountain. But Tien Pao's mother jumped up in the jeep, and in the fierce strength of her joy she lifted Tien Pao high and screamed a terrible scream at the mountain. 'It is Tien Pao! It is Tien Pao!'

Her cry rang up the mountainside. Men stopped and looked down, and one man halfway up the rocky hill let his huge sledge hammer fall from his hand. He just stood. But then he bellowed it out: 'It is Tien Pao!'

He came plunging down. He came straight down, straight toward the jeep. He used no paths. But he could not run that fast, not down a mountain. He fell. He struggled up again, and fell. He leaped up. All round him the men were shouting at him, running toward him. He half turned to them as he lunged on. 'It is Tien Pao,' he bellowed, and that answered all and explained all, and he came on in terrible, plunging strides.

Tien Pao's mother sank down on the seat, her strength suddenly all gone. Her whole body trembled, she clung fiercely to Tien Pao, and she cried. Softly she cried, and Tien Pao cried with her as they watched his plunging father. And in his happiness he had to tell Lieutenant Hamsun, who could not

160

understand. 'Oh, it was my mother, and I knew it. She had been on the revetment, but they called the younger women down to pull the roller to finish the job before dark. Oh, I knew it, I knew it. And my little sister is with neighbours in a little village near this airfield.' Suddenly he remembered his little pig. He grabbed up Glory-of-the-Republic, he hugged him.

And as Tien Pao finished talking, his mother looked and looked her gratitude at the lieutenant. 'It is Tien Pao,' she softly told the lieutenant as if it were a wholly new and unbelievable thing. 'It is Tien Pao.' And in her gratitude this timid, shy Chinese woman leaned forward and laid her hand on the lieutenant's arm and talked to him in earnest Chinese, and the tears rolled unheeded down her cheeks.

'It is Tien Pao,' she said again. 'And tomorrow and tomorrow and tomorrow—and all the days to come—there will still be my little son. And the house won't be too empty and the anxious heart too full . . . Ah, tomorrow, and tomorrow, and then will come a day when there will be no more shooting, and no more running from the shooting, and no war. There will come a day when the little family of Tien will go back to their village, and live in peace. Ah, tomorrow and tomorrow. Ah, ah, ah.'

She had no more words. She choked on them and her tears streamed. And there came his father, and his mother was clutching him fiercely again. There sat the lieutenant half turned, and he did not understand what his mother had said. Ah, but he did understand. He understood! The heart understands without words.

From The House of Sixty Fathers *by Meindert de Jong*

229   Luck? I

I have a round stone that I keep in my pocket and it brings me luck. It is fairly small and it is very smooth. When I rubbed it once I got chosen for the school football team. I kept it in my pocket when I took the eleven plus and I passed.

I always seem to do better at things if the stone is in my pocket, and I don't forget to rub it.

Stephen (aged 12)

230 Luck? II

Some children are not happy unless they can entice the correct answers on to their papers by means beyond the ordinary power of nature. They put their faith in new pencils which have never written a mistake; they clasp their thumbs ('this is very lucky,' says a Brixton boy); they cross their fingers or touch wood that an answer they have written down is correct.

From The Lore and Language of Schoolchildren *by Iona and Peter Opie*

231 Barren Creek's Christmas Gifts

The trail was hot and dusty and the drops of blood which fell from the wounded man were soon covered over by the dust. The man lay forward across the horse's neck. He was almost unconscious.

Walter saw the wounded man's horse approaching just as he was about to make his camp for the night. He ran to help.

'Water!' gasped the stranger. Walter helped him from the horse and made him comfortable on the ground, propped against a saddle. After he had a drink the stranger caught Walter's wrist and spoke fiercely.

'You've got to help. There are two bags of gold in my saddlebag. It's to get Christmas provisions for the people of Barren Creek. If they don't get them they might even starve, but on the way a gang of outlaws . . .'

The stranger's voice tailed away as his head fell forward. He was dead.

Walter buried him and then got the bags of gold. He was just a poor cowboy and he had never seen so much money. He could be rich for life! Nobody even knew he had the money.

'Don't be stupid,' he said to himself, 'what a Christmas those people will have if they don't get that food.' He rested until dawn and then set off for the town of Pinto which was two days ride away. It was a very worrying ride because Walter kept thinking about the outlaws.

At Pinto Walter got the provisions and a wagon and another man to help him. They rode to Barren Creek and got there on Christmas Eve. The people there were sorry to hear of the death of their friend but they were very relieved to see the food.

One of the townsmen stepped forward and held up his hands.

'Friends,' he said, 'this town needs more than this food, it needs a sheriff, and who better than this brave, honest man here.'

A great cheer went up. Walter became Barren Creek's first sheriff. After Christmas he rounded up the gang of outlaws who had murdered the lonely horseman.

James (aged 11)

232   The Chess Match

The stone went scudding away over the pavement as Jimmy fired an imaginary shot wide of the goalkeeper's left hand. The sight of a small cut in the leather of the toe cap of his shoe brought him quickly back to reality. Guiltily he stopped and rubbed the toe of his shoe on the sock of his other leg.

Suddenly the bag of shopping seemed much heavier and he felt very hungry. Ah well, the sooner he got this lot up-stairs the sooner he would get some peanut butter and bread to fill up on.

Turning into the dirty staircase he began the long climb to the fourth floor. As he passed along the landings he heard snatches of televised noise from behind some of the doors. The Jones' had pop blaring out as usual, probably that Marcia he thought.

When he reached the dark green door with the white plastic seven on it, and the dirt-outlined 'three' where the plastic figure was missing, he banged it hard with his knee.

'It's our Jim,' yelled four-year-old Julie as she looked through the letterbox before opening the door.

'Let him in then Duck,' called Mum's voice as the door opened in slow jerks with Julie swinging on the other side of it.

'Leave off that door, Julie,' Mum called. 'Good lad Jim. We'll soon have some tea now.'

Mum was busy by the sink and Jimmy noticed that she hadn't even taken her mac off yet. Sometimes it worried him to see her pushing her hair out of her eyes in that tired way she had. She never mentioned Dad but Jimmy guessed how much she missed him.

Catching him looking at her, Mum gave one of those smiles which always made him feel better. The little lines crinkled round the corners of her eyes.

'I haven't forgotten, Jim' she said. 'Chess night isn't it? Soon as I get these beans opened we'll be ready for tea. Betsy have you got that table laid?'

Betsy's voice came piping out of the other room but Jimmy didn't hear it. Chess. Those black and white squares and the pieces moving about on them like a battle swaying this way and that. To think he'd once thought those little 'uns were called prawns and those fine knights were horses!

Half an hour later he was up in old Mrs Knight's flat. Every Wednesday at six he went up and she was always ready for him, with the board laid out and the pieces standing there stiff and straight as if daring anyone to move them badly.

'Ha, Jim,' Mrs Knight always greeted him the same way with her slow whispering voice. Two peppermints lay on his side of the board and two lay behind hers. Every week, when he hadn't seen her for a bit, Jimmy thought how really old she looked. Her hair was so thin and straggly and there were such great big blue veins on her tiny hands.

'You're white.' Old Mrs Knight interrupted his thoughts and waved him to his place with a bony finger. Unwrapping one of the peppermints she waited for him to start. Moving his king's pawn the traditional two squares forward Jimmy settled comfortably into the faded old arm chair. The game was on.

Two hours later with a cackle of delight old Mrs Knight slid her rook down to join her queen in adjacent squares and Jim saw the checkmate before she even said it.

'Oh but you're getting better, me lad,' she wheezed as she stood up. 'Oh my, you are.'

Five minutes later she set down the tray with the two mugs of boiling water on it. Dropping a tea bag into each mug she then pulled the lid off the round tin which Jim knew would be half full of ginger snaps. They had two biscuits each with their tea then Jimmy stood up to go.

'Goodnight Jimmy,' said old Mrs Knight. 'See you next week, Son.'

As Jimmy walked off along the landing he thought of all their great battles. He knew he was getting better and his mind went back to those first games. It had all started when he was being nosey and looking in through the old lady's kitchen window. She'd been playing chess by herself but instead of chasing him away she'd asked him in. That was the beginning of it.

Next day at school it was chess club at dinner time and Jimmy's victory gave him another two points towards the term's championship. For somebody who'd never been much good at anything at school, the chess club was like a day at the seaside, fish and chips, and staying up late all rolled into one for him. Mr Evans, who ran it, knew how much it meant to Jimmy but even he didn't know about old Mrs Knight.

The days passed by until it was Wednesday again. When he got home and unlocked the door Mum's shopping list was on the table under a milk bottle with the pound note beside it. Going down the stairs and out into the rain Jim could feel the impatience beginning already. He was black tonight and if he got his queen out early . . .

By the time he got back with the shopping he could feel the water seeping through the worn sole of his right shoe. When Julie let him in as usual he put the bag down in the middle of the kitchen floor and blew the wet hair out of his eyes. It was then that he noticed how quiet it was. Mum was at the sink as usual but none of the kids were chasing about.

'Shopping Mum,' said Jim. The only reply was 'Hmmmm,' and Jimmy thought that the breakfast washing-up seemed to be taking an unusual amount of concentration. He wasn't used to such a quiet house so to do something about it he began to whistle 'We shall not be moved' as he went to change his socks. He'd just got one foot on the stairs when he saw the parcel.

It was a very untidy parcel, made up mainly of torn bits of brown paper held together with small pieces of Sellotape. On one side of it, written in block capitals with a Biro, was his name.

'Not a birthday, not Christmas, how come I've got this?' Jimmy muttered to himself as he peeled off one corner of the wrapping. Soon all the brown paper was off and Jimmy found himself looking at the familiar box.

The pieces lay there, black on one side, white on the other, stiff and proud. They were his now, he realised. As he looked at the crumpled wrapping paper and heard the chink of cups from the kitchen he got slowly to his feet. He didn't feel like making any noise now either.

Redvers Brandling

233   The Bus

The bus, a 279, was travelling along its route the same as ever. I was coming home from work not in a particularly good mood because the union wanted us to go on strike, and I had little enough money as it was.

The bus halted at a request stop and one of those long-haired layabouts climbed on. He was dressed in filthy-looking clothes and just watching him turned my stomach over. His hair was long and greasy and generally revolting.

When the bus conductor asked for his fare the layabout reached into his pocket and put on a false look of complete surprise. He searched through all of his pockets and announced that he had left his wallet at home. What absolute rubbish!

Paul (aged 12)

234

Dear Editors,

The dinners at my school are not horrible but they are not nice either. I only stay to dinner because my mum has got a job. I have a suggestion. Could we have a canteen and buy our own food? At the moment we have our dinner in a large classroom (which we call the hall). We have a few dinner ladies. We have two sittings, so you can guess second sitting get more. On days when we can have something which we like we can only have a little bit, and on days when it's 'ugh' you have a lot.

From a junior school magazine

235   New Boy

My first sight of All Saints School was on a warm spring morning in early May. I didn't think much of it I might tell you. It was small and there was a decayed look about it. After

Highfield Primary it was enough to make anybody feel homesick.

Still it was no use thinking like that. My father had got a better job here, we'd already moved into our new house and this was going to be my new school whether I liked it or not. Mum pushed open the door and we stepped into a tiny entrance hall. Another door opened into a corridor and the first room was labelled 'Headmaster'.

Well to cut a long story short I sat there while the adults talked away as usual.

'Should be a great asset, Mrs Pearce, hmm, very good report from his last school, hm.' He was all 'hmms' that headmaster. Then suddenly Mum's gone and I'm being ushered into a large, gloomy room.

'Another one I'm afraid, Bill,' says the headmaster to a teacher, in a voice he mistakenly thinks I can't hear. Then turning to me, 'This is your new teacher, Simon. His name is Mr Watson '

The first week wasn't too bad. All Saints was a small school after Highfield and there were only four classes. New kids were such a rarity that I got the feeling they were queuing up to see me on that first day, but after that they mostly left me to myself. Then it happened. They found out about me.

Now perhaps I should have told you at the start about my memory. I don't know why, but it's like a fly paper, and all those facts and figures that teachers love just stick to it like flies. 'Where was the Battle of Hastings fought?' 'What is the capital of New Zealand?' 'How many sides has an icosahedron?' The answers to questions like that and loads of others I can remember without even trying. 'Marvellous', you say, but it isn't, you know, and after that first week the same old trouble started again.

It was after the maths lesson on the second Monday when Gary strolled up to me in the playground.

'Bit of a brainbox aren't you?'

Short and tough, Gary was the sort of boy I'd rather have for a friend than an enemy any day.

'No, not really, Gary. Some things just sort of stick in my memory, you know.'

I tried to be friendly and casual but of course it didn't work.

'We don't like show-offs. Made old Wattie's day with all that squared this and squared that stuff didn't you?'

He didn't say any more but turned and suddenly let out a great yell and ran off to where a game of cricket was just starting. The other boys all milled round him and I was left standing by myself. Nobody else spoke to me during that playtime.

After that it got worse. Nobody bothered to speak to me, not even the girls. If we had teams in PE I was always the last one to be picked. My plimsolls kept disappearing from the PE rack and turning up in the toilets or on the playing field. I tried giving old Wattie the wrong answers and missing off the 'Sir' when I spoke to him but it didn't seem to make any difference.

Of course I still did well at all the work because I just can't help that, you see. This went on for a few weeks and then one morning in maths I looked up and saw Wattie gazing at me in a funny way.

'Look this way a minute. All of you!' he said in that dry sort of way he used.

'Now you know we've been studying plans for our new school extensions this term; well I've asked the builders if we can go out on to the site this morning and see how they are getting on. I thought perhaps while we were out there we'd have a little competition and see who's the strongest man in the class.'

This was quite a speech from Wattie and it caused a stir of excitement in the class. One or two of the girls tittered as Gary flexed his muscles. We put our books away and went out over the playground.

On the site it was really interesting and soon everybody forgot about the strong man stuff as Mr Watson and one of the builders talked to us and showed us how to mix cement, lay bricks, fit door frames and use a spirit level. Then we came to a box full of bricks and Wattie stopped beside it.

'This is it,' he said, 'strong man contest. Who's going to try and lift it?'

Well Gary and Ivor Green and a few others tried but although there was a lot of gasping and groaning nobody could get more than one end of the box off the ground.

'Are you going to have a try, Simon?' asked Mr Watson, and again I thought what a funny look he was giving me.

'Yes sir,' I said, for I had seen what I was looking for. I quickly picked up the long thick plank of wood which was lying nearby, and then I laid it over the rubble-filled tin drum which lay on its side near the box of bricks. Easing the box up a bit at a time I managed to get one end of the plank under it. Then I went round to the other end of the plank which was sticking up in the air over the drum. I pressed on it with all my strength and slowly the box of bricks rose a few inches off the ground.

A funny thing happened then. Some of the class started to clap and after a second they were all clapping. Old Wattie held up his hand. I thought he was going to say something about 'the principle of the lever' but he didn't you know. Instead he just said, 'That's it then, strong man Simon Pearce. In you go, all of you.'

Everybody turned to go in and suddenly I wasn't on my own any more. They were all round me grinning and saying, 'That was great,' and 'Good lad, Si.' Then Gary was beside me feeling the muscles in my arm and giving me a playful punch as he said, 'That was a good maths lesson, wasn't it?'

As we walked in I kept thinking how lucky it was that the plank and drum had been just in the right spot. How lucky, how . . . suddenly I looked round at old Wattie. He was looking straight at me and I've often wondered if he got something in his eye at that moment, or did he really wink?

Redvers Brandling

170

236 Litter

Litter is a result of our slovenly throw-away attitude encouraged by 'disposable' goods. It is also an attitude that has to change. Don't litter. It's as simple as that. No one appreciates litter on the landscape. Keep Britain Tidy Group estimates that more than twenty million pounds a year is spent on litter collection.

Show your respect for the land by making sure that you make no contribution to the litter that despoils it.

Carry a litter bag in your car and use it.

Make sure that rubbish cannot escape from your dustbin, even on a windy day.

Never dump rubbish illegally; report any violations of dumping that you see.

Be willing to pick up other people's litter. If you have the courage, retrieve litter and return it to the litterbug on the spot. You can ask him if he 'forgot' to pick it up himself.

Participate in clean-up campaigns and help to organise them.

Jonathan Holliman

237 Prisoners *

It was January when they had first come to Stalag Luft III, and for the whole of that month the ground was under snow. Snow lay thickly on the roofs of the barrack blocks and gave an air of gaiety to the barbed wire which sparkled and glittered in the sun. Every post carried its cap of crisp, powdery snow, and when the wind blew, the snow drifted up against the coiled wire, softening its gauntness. Escape in this weather was impossible, and when the snow stopped falling the prisoners

* The above extract is the Introduction to *The Wooden Horse* (published by Collins) in which the author, Eric Williams, describes his escape from a German prison camp in 1943.

made a bobsleigh run and cut up their bed boards to make toboggans. They flooded the football pitch and made an ice rink on which they skated from morning until evening. The camp was pure and clean while the snow lay on the ground, and the air loud with the shouts of the skaters. It was only when the night carts came to empty the aborts that the compound became offensive, and the air was malodorous, and long, yellow streaks marked the white snow where the carts had been.

When the thaw came the camp was a sea of mud. The packed ice of the toboggan run was the last to melt, and the skating rink was a miniature lake on which a few enthusiasts sailed their home-made yachts. Then that dried up and the football pitch was reconditioned. The goalposts were replaced and the earth dams that had held the water were removed.

With the spring came the renewed interest in escape. Spring is the escaping season. Peter and John had already escaped once from their previous camp, only to be brought back after two days of wandering aimlessly around the Polish countryside. That had been in the winter when the country was bare and cold and they had been exhausted and almost glad to be recaptured and brought back into the camp.

As the weather grew warmer they were ready to try again. For weeks now they had been thinking of starting a tunnel. But all the possible starting places had been used before.

The camp was set in a clearing of the pine forest; a few single-storey wooden barracks raised on piles three feet above the ground, huddled together inside the wire; the wire itself, the main feature of the camp, strong and heavily interlaced, a twelve foot double fence of bristling spikes. There were arc lamps hanging above the wire and at intervals along each fence stood 'goon boxes', small sentry boxes on stilts higher than the wire. These goon boxes were armed with machine guns and carried searchlights which swept the camp continually during the hours of darkness. There were two guards in each box, connected by telephone to the main guardroom at the prison gates. 'Posten' carrying tommy guns patrolled the wire between the sentry boxes.

Fifteen feet inside the main fence was a single strand of barbed wire twelve inches above the ground. This was the trip wire and anyone stepping over it was shot at by the guards. A narrow pathway trodden by the feet of the prisoners ran round the camp just inside the trip wire. This was their exercise ground, known as the circuit. It had become a convention in the camp to walk only in an anti-clockwise direction round the circuit.

The surface of the compound was a mixture of sand, powdered leaf mould and dirt, which in the summer formed a thick layer of soft dust sometimes blown by the wind into a blinding cloud which hung like a pall across the camp. In the winter this dust was churned by the prisoners' feet into a grey sea of clinging mud.

Under this top layer the subsoil was clean, hard yellow sand.
Yellow when damp, but drying to a startling whiteness in the
sun. The Germans knew that every tunnel carried its
embarrassment of excavated sand and viewed each disturbance
of this grey upper layer with suspicion. Every excavation made
for a drain, rubbish pit or garden was carefully watched by the
ferrets, or security guards. It was only by elaborate camouflage
that the tell-tale yellow sand could be hidden in these places.
The skin of grey dust formed one of the most effective defences
of the camp.

From The Wooden Horse *by Eric Williams*

238 A Peaceful Solution

'Alas,' said the space-bat-angel-dragon, 'I am useless. Utterly
useless. All we do in space is fly, or make music.'

'Make music?' asked the Iron Man. 'How? What sort of
music?'

'Haven't you heard of the music of the spheres?' asked the
dragon. 'It's the music that space makes to itself. All the spirits
inside all the stars are singing. I'm a star spirit. I sing too. The
music of the spheres is what makes space so peaceful.'

'Then whatever made you want to eat up the earth?' asked the
Iron Man. 'If you're all so peaceful up there, how did you get
such greedy and cruel ideas?'

The dragon was silent for a long time after this question. And
at last he said: 'It just came over me. I don't know why. It just
came over me, listening to the battling shouts and the war cries
of the earth—I got excited, I wanted to join in.'

'Well, you can sing for us instead,' said the Iron Man. 'It's a
long time since anybody here on earth heard the music of the
sphere. It might do us all good.'

And so it was fixed. The space-bat-angel-dragon was to send
his star back to the constellation of Orion, and he was to live

inside the moon. And every night he was to fly around the earth, through the heavens, singing.

So his fearful shape, slowly swimming through the night sky, didn't frighten people, because it was dark and he couldn't be seen. But the whole world could hear him, a strange soft music that seemed to fill the whole of space, a deep weird singing, like millions of voices singing together.

Meanwhile the Iron Man was the world's hero. He went back to his scrap yard. But now everybody in the world sent him a present. Some only sent him a nail. Some sent him an old car. One rich man even sent him an ocean liner. He sprawled there in his yard, chewing away, with his one ear slightly drooped where the white heat of that last roasting had slightly melted it. As he chewed, he hummed in harmony to the singing of his tremendous slave in heaven.

And the space-bat-angel's singing had the most unexpected effect. Suddenly the world became wonderfully peaceful. The singing got inside everybody and made them as peaceful as starry space, and blissfully above all their earlier little squabbles. The strange soft eerie space-music began to alter all the people of the world. They stopped making weapons. The countries began to think how they could live pleasantly alongside each other. All they wanted to do was to have peace to enjoy this strange, wild, blissful music from the giant singer in space.

From The Iron Man *by Ted Hughes*

239   The Well-off Kid

Two new patients were admitted to the Children's Ward of the General Hospital that morning. One was called Harry, and the other Hilary.

Harry was carried in on a stretcher, covered with a grey blanket, and a large hot-water bottle at his feet. Along with him came his elder brother, Eric, a boy of ten, to see young Harry safely handed over and all particulars taken down.

The patient, who was seven, was wearing patched flannel trousers and a green cotton jersey. He was removed from the stretcher as he was and gently slipped into bed between two blankets, until the doctor had examined him. Nurse Broyce took his pulse and temperature, and then Eric told her the name and address, and gave a brief account of the accident. They had been playing football in the street, and in a furious attempt to save a goal, Harry had either run into a car or the car had run into him.

Harry himself, a little scratched and bruised, said nothing until his brother was leaving, then he suddenly sat up and piped out: 'There ain't nothin' wrong with me!'

'I'm sure there isn't,' said Nurse Broyce, 'but they won't take our word. You'll have to let the doctor see you.'

Again he called out, as Eric was waving to him from the door, 'Don't forget to tell Mum, tell her there ain't a bally thing wrong with me. Say they just brought me in for a rest.'

At that moment the doctor arrived. 'There won't be much resting for you, young man,' he said. 'These nurses need some one to help serve the food.'

'I'm willin',' said Harry, looking round and grinning. It was then the second patient came in.

Hilary entered the ward accompanied by his parents, after a delayed farewell to his two aunts at the door. His father carried a pile of toys and books for the boy's amusement. The operation he had come to have was a simple one. His ears stuck out—commonly known as 'bat ears'—and in a week or so he would be going out with them pressed neatly to the sides of his head. His mother and a nurse took him to the bathroom to change, and he was settled into a bed next to Harry. But as his parents were leaving he suddenly set up a howl, and it was all the father could do to restrain the mother from taking him home again, or having him removed to a private ward. But finally the door closed on the parents, and after a time the ward settled down.

'Those two, Hilary and Harry,' remarked Nurse Smith to Nurse Broyce that evening, 'are the same age to the very day. But in every other way they seem as unlike each other as two kids could be.'

Harry had short hair, wiry and black, while Hilary had blond, wavy locks. Harry's small, eager eyes were watching all that was going on, while Hilary's large, unhappy eyes stared at the ceiling.

'Well, Hilary,' said Nurse Broyce, 'I think we'd better be putting your books and toys away. Would you like something to read before "lights out"?'

Hilary shook his head and whispered, 'No thank you, Nurse.'

She turned to Harry. 'Now what have you got there, Harry?' she asked.

Harry produced his only toy. 'It's my rabbit's foot, Nurse,' he said. 'It don't half bring me luck.'

'You'll need it,' she said, 'if you keep on playing football in the street.'

'Naughty, wasn't I?' said Harry.

A whimper was heard from the next bed. Harry turned to him. 'Just think of the fun we'll have if they keep us here till Christmas.'

'Christmas!' exclaimed Hilary in a shocked whisper. 'So long!'

'You never know your luck,' said Harry. 'My Eric was in hospital one Christmas—told us all how smashin' it was.'

'Have you any brothers, Hilary?' asked Nurse Broyce.

'No, Nurse,' said Hilary, 'there's only me.'

'I've three brothers,' said Harry, then added 'and one sister. 'Course I ain't seen her yet—my sister.'

'Oh,' Nurse Broyce tucked him in. 'And how's that, Harry?'

'Because she ain't been born yet,' said Harry.

At this piece of news even Hilary sat up and took notice.

'But you can't know whether you've a sister or not,' he said, 'until she's born.'

'My mum,' said Harry firmly, 'has promised us a sister. She's going to have a baby any day now.'

'But that doesn't follow that it will be a sister,' said Hilary. 'Does it, Nurse?'

Harry didn't wait for the Nurse's opinion. 'When my mum promises us something,' he said, 'she sees we get it. So I've got three brothers, and a sister to come. Got me?'

Hilary hesitated. 'Oh, I see,' he said. 'Uh, good night.'

'Good night, mate. Good night, Nurse.'

'Good night, Nurse,' said Hilary. Something about Harry seemed to have infected him, and he was already settling in.

Harry's diagnosis of himself proved quite sound. In three days his bruises were out and his scratches healing, and he was ready for discharge. He was serving the morning milk drinks in the ward, and waiting for someone to collect him, when Eric arrived.

'Mum was sorry she couldn't come, Nurse,' said Eric, 'so she asked me to thank you for all you'd done. She had a baby last night.'

'Well, how nice,' said the Nurse. 'And is everybody well?'

'Oh, fine,' said Eric. 'Lovely baby, weighs—'

Hilary called out excitedly: 'What is it—boy or a girl?'

'Why,' said Eric, 'it's a boy.'

'What did I tell you Harry?' called out Hilary. 'Just because your mother promised you a sister it didn't mean you would have one.'

178

At that moment Nurse Broyce felt very sorry for Harry. But it was clear that Harry didn't feel sorry for himself. He went across to Hilary's bed and smiled at him.

'It don't have to be this time, Hilary,' he said. 'My mum's promised us a sister—she'll see we get one.' His tone carried utter conviction. 'So now I've four brothers, and a sister to come.' He put out his hand, and the two boys shook hands. 'I reckon them ears'll look a treat when they take them bandages off, mate. I'll have to come in one day an' have mine done. So long, Hilary. Good luck. Good-bye, everybody, good-bye.'

Nurse Broyce saw Harry out to the steps, and kissed him good-bye. On her way back she met Nurse Smith, who was just coming on duty after a day off.

'Young Harry just left,' she said.

'Harry?' said Nurse Smith. 'Was Harry the well-off kid?'

Nurse Broyce thought for a moment. 'Yes,' she said, 'Harry was well-off.'

As Nurse Smith opened the ward door she saw Hilary sitting up wiping his eyes. She turned to Nurse Broyce. 'Hey, Broyce, thought you said that the well-off kid had left!'

'He has,' said Nurse Broyce. 'I mean young Harry.'

'Do you call him well off?' said Nurse Smith.

'Yes, I do,' said Nurse Broyce. 'He came in here full of cheer and good faith, and he spread them all around the place. Those are things money can't buy. And if young Harry isn't well off, nobody ever was!'

And with that she went across to the empty bed, whipped off the sheets and blankets and began to prepare it for the next patient.

Bill Naughton

240   Echo Valley

Do you know what an echo is? There are some places where, if you make a noise, the sound comes bouncing back to you. For instance, if you were in a rock-walled cave or climbing up a mountain you might shout and hear your words repeated several times.

In Switzerland, near Grindelwald, there is a valley aptly named Echo Valley. A story is told of a small boy—we will call him John—who was taken there by his mother. As he did not know what an echo was, she explained it to him by pretending that there was another boy up in the mountains who would answer if John called. 'Go on, try,' she said. So John shouted as loudly as he could, 'Hullo.' Back came the answer, 'Hullo . . . Hullo . . . Hullo . . .' 'Who are you?' shouted John. 'Who are you . . . Who are you . . . Who are you . . .' came the reply. John thought that this was rather rude, so he yelled back, 'I don't like you.' 'I don't like you . . . I don't like you . . . I don't like you . . .' the echo replied.

This was too much for John, who began to cry. His mother said, 'Cheer up, you were a bit rude, weren't you? Try being friendly and see what happens.' So John wiped away his tears and shouted, 'I want to be friends with you . . . Let's play a game,' said John, and it appeared that the boy in the mountain wanted to play too. After that, John had a fine time calling to his 'friend', the echo.

Have you noticed that what happened to John in Echo Valley is something like what happens to us in daily life? For example, if your brother or sister annoys you and you say, 'I hate you,' like the echo, they will probably reply, 'And I hate you too.' Or if you pinch someone, he will probably pinch you back— harder! You then hit him and he hits you, and so it goes on, most likely ending up with both of you in tears. On the other hand, if you are friendly, kind and polite to other people, they usually respond in the same way. Try smiling sometimes when you speak: it is surprising how difficult folk will find it not to smile back.

John D. Searle

241 The Garden

It all started when Jimmy saw Mum reading the magazine. Usually she read magazines with pictures of ladies in woolly cardigans on the front. But this one was different. It was full of pictures of spades and tools and lawn-mowers.

'What are you reading mum?' asked Jimmy.

Mum smiled and pushed a stray piece of hair out of her eyes. Jimmy thought she looked sad for some reason.

'Just a magazine,' she answered.

'It's not like those you usually read,' said Jimmy.

'No, well you see it's Daddy's birthday the day after next,' said Mum, 'and I'm looking to see if I can find anything he would like.'

'Oh,' said Jimmy. He looked over Mum's shoulder at the magazine and then he looked at her again. Now he knew why she was sad. It was all those pictures of lawn mowers.

Since the family had moved into this block of flats Jimmy had often heard Dad say how much he missed their old garden.

'Look,' he would say, picking Jimmy up and putting him on his shoulders. 'Nowhere to plant even a cabbage down there.'

And Jimmy would look through the window and down to where all the cars and buses moved about like Dinky toys.

'Jimmy,' Mum's voice interrupted his thoughts. 'It's tea time. Come on. I've got some of your favourite cream buns.'

The magazine about the lawn mowers was under the television set and Mum had her cheerful face on now.

'Smashing Mum,' said Jimmy. But all the same he hadn't forgotten about Dad's birthday and that garden.

It was after he and Mum had been out shopping the next morning that he had the idea. When they moved to the flat Dad had used two wooden boxes to carry things in. Afterwards he had taken them to pieces and put them in the storeroom downstairs.

'Mum can I get some of Dad's wood?'

'All right dear,' said Mum, 'but what do you want it for?'

'Just to make something.'

Mum unlocked the storeroom. The door was a bright blue colour and it had silver numbers saying 'twenty seven' on it.

'What a mess,' sighed Mum as they looked at the pile of suitcases, Jimmy's old pushchair and the sledge. But Jimmy could see what he wanted.

When they got back upstairs Jimmy took the pieces of wood into his bedroom. Then he got some newspaper from Mum and spread it on the floor. Next he got the tools Dad had given him for Christmas. Soon he was very busy with his hammer and nails.

That night Mum rang up Gran as she did every Wednesday. She always let Jimmy speak to Gran too.

'Is that you Jimmy?' said Gran, the way she always did.

'Yes,' said Jimmy. 'Will you get me something Gran?'

'Oh, what's that then?' asked Gran.

Jimmy quickly told Gran what he wanted. He did this because Mum had gone off into the kitchen to switch the kettle off and he didn't want her to hear.

The next day was Dad's birthday. Mum made a special tea and she said Dad was going to get all his presents then. Gran arrived at dinner time.

'Whatever have you got there?' said Mum as she let Gran in.

'Never you mind,' said Gran in between puffs and gasps. She carried the heavy looking shopping bag to Jimmy's bedroom. Opening the door in front of her, he followed her inside.

When tea time came Dad was back. He had a special cake, and he and Mum and Gran all laughed at the candles which spelled out 'DAD'. He got a pair of slippers from Gran and a new pipe from Mum. Jimmy didn't say anything until Dad had finished looking at these presents.

'Dad.'

'Yes Jimmy.'

'I've got something for you.'

'Have you? That's lovely Jimmy.'

'It's in my bedroom.'

'Come on then, what are we waiting for?'

Whizzing Jimmy round in his arms Dad went to the bedroom. Gran, smiling, and Mum looking very puzzled, followed.

'There,' said Jimmy flinging open the door.

'Why,' said Dad,' it's just what I wanted. It's a . . . it's a garden!'

Jimmy looked at the box he'd made. It was filled with the soil Gran had brought. Then he saw the white packet she had brought too.

'Daddy,' said Jimmy. 'Gran said it wouldn't be a very good garden for growing cabbages. But she said you would like these.'

He gave Dad the white packet. 'Marigolds' it had written on it.

Redvers Brandling

242   The Sea Changes Everything

For ten minutes the boy they called 'Jacknife' had sat facing a blank page in his English exercise book. Normally he enjoyed writing stories: it was something people said he did well, and his teachers at the other school always read them out to the rest of the class or put them in the school magazine.

But in the old school they had called him by his proper name, Colin. That was a year ago. What was it his dad would have said, if he'd been alive? 'There's a lot of water gone under the bridge since then, lad.'

Jacknife. Stupid sort of name to get given, really, he thought. All he'd done to earn it was one of his special dives in the swimming pool they went to once a week. Everyone had come laughing and clapping round the springboard as his face broke the surface.

'It's called a Jacknife dive,' he said. 'It's easy. You touch your toes in mid-air, and then straighten out before you hit the water.'

So the name stuck. He didn't mind, really. He looked out of the window and saw the tall, finger-thin chimneys of the new town his mother had brought him to when his father died and remembered how clean the air had been as it swept in on the south-east breeze across the estuary. A long way from the smoke-filled area they called the Midlands.

Here there were no white horses sweeping in from the North Sea and turning themselves into hissing snakes as they broke on the brown sand of the beach. No fishing boats ducking their chins down into the breakers. No seagulls screaming and soaring like living kites over the bay.

Funny, he thought. Here I am sitting facing a blank sheet of paper. I've been asked to write a story about the sea. The other kids in the class probably don't know what the sea looks like, tastes like when you swallow it, feels like when you throw yourself into the rollers.

How it sparkles when the sun hits it, growls like thunder when the wind gets to Force Eight and calms down like a sheet of plastic when the gale drops. And I can't even get started.

'What's the matter, Jacknife?' asked his teacher, Mr O'Connor. 'Got cramp in your writing hand? Can't you think of anything to say about the sea?'

Jacknife looked up slowly and grinned. Good bloke, O'Connor. Never nagged at you like some of the other teachers.

'Trouble is, sir,' he said, 'I can think of too much.'

'Ah,' said Mr O'Connor. 'Well, we'll look forward to reading it. That's when you get it done. Or if you get it done.' He went back to his desk.

They used to get lots of visitors at the seaside town where Jacknife had been born, and every year dozens of them would go plunging into the sea as if it was one big watery joke. Jacknife and his friends would stand on the beach and laugh at them dipping their white chicken skins into breakers and grin at the goose pimples on their London-bred bodies when they came out shivering.

That's if they came out—for lots of them would ignore the signs which said 'Danger' and dive in at ebb-tide and get caught by the treacherous current which swept eastwards like a mill-race. Many of them would be drowned every year, washed up on the marshes round the point of land the locals called Foulness. Lots of mothers would go back home to London without their children and the smiles they had brought with them. Somehow people didn't learn to treat the sea with respect.

And the way the grown-ups used to talk! They said loudly that the tide was coming in or going out. But seamen, and Colin and his friends, called it 'flooding' or 'ebbing'. The visitors thought you got spring tides only at spring-time. But you got them, really, twice a month when the moon was full or new, and the sea would threaten to come over the wall into the road.

186

Neap-tides, or 'nips' as his father used to call them, came in between.

But his father got caught himself by the sea. His fishing boat went out on a flood-tide one day—a Friday, when sailors said you should stay on shore—and a blustery sou'wester blew up over the Dogger and somehow or other his boat turned turtle and whole crew got drowned.

He learnt the dive which had earned him his new name by looking down at the water far below the barge pier, gritting his teeth and taking a deep breath and flinging himself far out into the green gap below.

He'd learnt to swim one day when he was seven. One moment he had a foot on the shingle (cheating really) and the next was somehow moving through the water with his arms flailing like paddles on a pleasure-steamer. As easy as that. And he got better at it. Could swim faster and farther than any of his pals, eventually.

He knew the estuary as he knew the crinkling lines on the palms of his hand. He knew how you could find cockles spitting up at you from the black mud, how you could find flounders trying to settle themselves cunningly deep into the sand as you tried to spear them, and how you could catch dirty great eels in the old pipes under the pier. They went to sleep in them, daft perishers.

Yes, he knew the sea. Or thought he did, anyway.

Then one afternoon he went down to the beach by himself, put his swimming trunks on quickly under a beach-hut, trod over the pebbles and threw himself into the water. He'd been going about by himself lately since his father hadn't made his landfall, and his pals were leaving him alone till he got over it.

It was cold, the sea. Nobody else fancied it. The visitors were all huddled up under blankets in their deck-chairs.

He struck out with a crawl stroke. All he wanted to do was to lose himself in the greyness of the sea and wash off some of the depression he'd had the last week or so. He swam until his arms ached, and then turned over on his back and floated with his hands splayed out on the water like a starfish. The sky was blue, with high banks of white-wool cloud building up over the headland. Somewhere a gull screamed sadly like a spoilt child.

And then he suddenly knew that the ebb-tide had got him in its treacherous arms. He was drifting farther and farther eastwards.

He struck out as hard as he could for the shore-line. It looked miles away. How could he have been so daft? After all he and his friends had said about the visitors?

His arms got heavier and he couldn't seem to get enough air into his lungs. He was swallowing more and more water and he felt sick. He knew he wasn't going to make it. It all seemed hopeless.

And the very moment this thought went through his mind he felt his body sink deeper down into the colder water just below the surface. He flung up one arm almost as if he was waving goodbye to everyone on the beach and gave up the struggle.

And all that business about having your whole life pass before your eyes as you drowned was a lot of old toffee. All you felt was a stomach-cramping fear that made you want to scream out loud and then your mouth filled with water and then you finally just felt that it was all such a great pity.

And the sea took you down as it had taken sailors: turned you into nothing from something in the way it turned rocks into sand and boulders into pebbles. It didn't care what you became. That was that.

And then he came to, lying on the sand being sick as a baby as someone leapt above him trying to pump air into his lungs. There was a crowd round him, and a lad a few years older than himself was saying something to him.

He'd seen Colin wave before he disappeared, he said, and he'd swum out, dived down and dragged him to the surface by his hair. He seemed to be angry. Colin could just make out what he was saying. 'You shouldn't go swimming when the tide's going out. It's dangerous.'

'Ebbing,' said Colin.

'Ebbing? What's that? Your name?' The visitors were crowding closer now, and Colin suddenly knew that the boy who had saved him must be one of them. 'No,' he said weakly, 'ebbing means going out.'

He heard the sound of an ambulance bell somewhere in the distance, and he knew he'd be all right. He closed his eyes, tireder than he'd ever felt in his life before.

When he woke up it was in a warm hospital bed, and his mother was leaning over him. She'd been crying, and who could blame her, thought Colin.

Soon after this they moved away from the seaport and went to live with his aunt in the grit and grime of the Midlands. The boy they now called Jacknife looked out of the window at the grey plumes of smoke drifting down from the factory chimneys and suddenly knew that it wasn't so bad after all. He picked up his pen and started to write.

Ronald Deadman

243

Saul spoke to Jonathan his son and all his household about killing David. But Jonathan was devoted to David and told him that his father Saul was looking for an opportunity to kill him. 'Be on your guard tomorrow morning,' he said, 'conceal yourself, and remain in hiding. Then I will come out and join my father in the open country where you are and speak to him about you, and if I discover anything I will tell you.' Jonathan spoke up for David to his father Saul and said to him, 'Sir, do not wrong your servant David; he has not wronged you; his conduct towards you has been beyond reproach. Did he not take his life in his hands when he killed the Philistine, and the Lord won a great victory for Israel? You saw it, you shared in the rejoicing; why should you wrong an innocent man and put David to death without cause?' Saul listened to Jonathan and swore solemnly by the Lord that David should not be put to death. So Jonathan called David and told him all this; then he brought him to Saul, and he was in attendance on the king as before.

War broke out again, and David attacked the Philistines and dealt them such a blow that they ran before him.

An evil spirit from the Lord came upon Saul as he was sitting in the house with his spear in his hand; and David was playing the harp. Saul tried to pin David to the wall with the spear, but he avoided the king's thrust so that Saul drove the spear into the wall. David escaped and got safely away.

1 Samuel XIX 1–10

244

And he told them this parable: 'There was a rich man whose land yielded heavy crops. He debated with himself: "What am I to do? I have no space to store my produce. This is what I will do," said he: "I will pull down my storehouses and build them bigger. I will collect in them all my corn and other goods, and then say to myself, 'Man, you have plenty of good things laid by, enough for many years: take life easy, eat, drink, and enjoy yourself.' " But God said to him, "You fool, this very night you must surrender your life; you have made your money—who will get it now?" That is how it is with the man who amasses wealth for himself and remains a pauper in the sight of God.'

Luke XII 16–21

245

'It is like a man going abroad, who called his servants and put his capital in their hands; to one he gave five bags of gold, to another two, to another one, each according to his capacity. Then he left the country. The man who had the five bags went at once and employed them in business, and made a profit of five bags, and the man who had the two bags made two. But the man who had been given one bag of gold went off and dug a hole in the ground, and hid his master's money. A long time afterwards their master returned, and proceeded to settle accounts with them. The man who had been given the five bags of gold came and produced the five he had made: "Master," he said, "you left five bags with me; look, I have made five more." "Well done, my good and trusty servant!" said the master. "You have proved trustworthy in a small way; I will now put you in charge of something big. Come and share your master's delight." The man with the two bags then came and said, "Master, you left two bags with me; look, I have made two more." "Well done, my good and trusty servant!" said the master. "You have proved trustworthy in a small way; I will now put you in charge of something big. Come and share your master's delight." Then the man who had been given one bag came and said, "Master, I knew you to be a hard man; you reap where you have not sown, you gather where you have not scattered; so I was afraid, and I went and hid your gold in the ground. Here it is—you have what belongs to you." "You lazy rascal!" said the master. "You knew that I reap where I have not sown, and gather where I have not scattered? Then you ought to have put my money on deposit, and on my return I should have got it back with interest. Take the bag of gold from him, and give it to the one with the ten bags." '

Matthew XXV 14–28

246

He looked up and saw the rich people dropping their gifts into the chest of the temple treasury; and he noticed a poor widow putting in two tiny coins. 'I tell you this,' he said: 'this poor widow has given more than any of them; for those others who have given had more than enough, but she, with less than enough, has given all she had to live on.'

Luke XXI 1–4

247   That Mad, Bad Badger by Molly Burkett

I thought this book was adorable. It was sad, thrilling, funny and adventurous. I'm sure you will love to read this book. I've read it twice and would read it again. I got this book from Chip Club but I'm sure it will be in the library soon because it is so popular.

Tina Sell (aged 11)

248   Cuffley Camp

I was in charge of the fire and in the morning the fire was out and I had to get it started again from the ashes. I used thin cardboard at first then gradually put on pieces of wood. I went to get some more fuel. Mr Evans showed me how to break up things for the fire by using an axe. In the afternoon I had to chop wood for the outdoor fire. Then at seven o'clock Mr Evans gave me some matches to light it. After a while the fire was burning very well and other schools came round our fire for a sing-song. It was good.

Adam (aged 10)

249 Choice

What is your favourite food?	Chinese.
Which country do your favourite stamps come from?	Canada.
What is your favourite colour?	Blue.
What is your favourite animal?	A cat.
What is your favourite book?	Hundreds of them.
What is your favourite plant?	Honeysuckle.
What would you like to be if you weren't a teacher?	
	A doctor.
Who is your favourite film star?	Robert Redford.

Laura Emerson and Janice May interview Mrs Keen for their junior school magazine

250 Education

The seventeenth century saw the foundation of two local charity schools . . . Robert Dewhurst purchased land in Churchgate from Robert Dacres of Cheshunt Great House and built the school there in 1640.

. . . The extant minutes of the trustees date from 1706, and until 1779 they give a picture of a succession of boys learning the three Rs, being tested by the trustees and finally leaving the school as apprentices. Not that the school was without its troubles, but these were minor until 1778 when the trustees interviewed complaining parents who alleged brutality by the master. The complaints can be summarised as follows:

James Etheridge had died from a kick in his belly. William Sale had been kicked and beaten with sticks twisted together. John Brown had a slate pencil pushed up his nose which caused 'a great bleeding'. Joseph Burr had had his arm twisted and had 'lost the use of it'. Benjamin Parrish had been struck on the temple and had died on the following day.

William Ward, the master, was given notice to leave 'at Michaelmas next', and this inadequate treatment is a comment on the cheapness with which the lives of the lower classes were held. There was however, a tightening up of regulations and more careful supervision by the trustees.

From Cheshunt in Hertfordshire *by Jack Edwards*

251   The Winning Goal

Our football team had a very bad start to the season. We drew with King's Road and Upshire and then we lost some matches by one goal.

When we played Pentbrook, the biggest school in the district we were soon a goal down. Then we got level with a goal from Joseph Barnas.

In the second half we were under considerable pressure. Our captain and goalie, Michael Blee, made some tremendous saves and Russell Jennings and Tony Barnas did a good job too.

Then we made a break. Joseph ran down the left wing and kicked to me. I outran one man but another was near me. He ran with me until I was on the edge of the penalty area.

Then I kicked the ball and to my surprise it went into the goal. I jumped with joy because there was only a minute to go to full time. When the whistle blew for the end of the match the team jumped for joy and lay down on the grass. We had won our first match.

Enrico Rodia (aged 11)

252   Manners or Manner?

The great secret, Eliza, is not having bad manners or good manners or any other particular sort of manners, but having the same manner for all human souls; in short, behaving as if you were in Heaven, where there are no third class carriages and one soul is as good as another.

George Bernard Shaw

253   Life in Victorian England

Two little girls, brought before a magistrate charged with being found begging, wept bitterly—explaining that unless they went out begging and brought home money their mothers would beat them and give them nothing to eat. While they begged in one place the mother of one of them went off on a begging round of her own, carrying a baby, returning from time to time to the children to collect what coppers they had gathered in. Most of the proceeds went on gin.

Late one night, crossing Westminster Bridge, a man heard a six year old girl pleading in terror with a great hulking fellow who was threatening to throw her over the parapet into the water. This passer-by reported what he had heard to a policeman, who went to investigate. It was discovered that the bully was a professional beggar of notoriously evil habits, an idle, dissolute vagabond who for years had been in the habit of buying children whom he took on tramps round the country for begging purposes. Nothing could be discovered about the parents of the little girl. Perhaps she had been stolen, perhaps she had been sold.

From Barnado: the Extraordinary Doctor *by Gladys Williams*

254   A Christmas Tale

I want to tell you a true story. Last Saturday my mum and I went Christmas shopping in London. We had to get presents for my sister, brother and dad. We were travelling on the train between Seven Sisters and Oxford Street. Suddenly as we got out of the train my mum said, 'My handbag's gone!'

We went to see a policeman and he said that there had been some stealing of handbags going on. My mum had some money in her pocket for us to get home. I felt very miserable because we could not buy our presents and I had even lost all my money as well. This was because it was in my mum's handbag.

When we got home my dad said we ought to ring up the stations to see if anybody had found the bag. He was worried because the bag had a lot of money in it and a cheque book and the keys to the house. We tried to forget about it. My mum wrote a letter to the Railway Lost Property Office the next day.

On Thursday of this week we got a card. It was from Baker Street Lost Property Office. It said: 'We have some property which might be yours. Bring this card to claim it.'

My mum went there next day while I was at school. They had her handbag. It still had all her money in it, all her papers and even her little pencil. She would have liked to give a reward to the honest person who found her bag but they didn't even say who they were.

My dad said, 'Never mind the money. That's the nicest Christmas story I have heard for a long time.'

Betty (aged 10)

255   Local 'Good Neighbour' Scheme

The local clergy and ministers have been exploring the possibility of setting up some kind of 'Good Neighbour' scheme, not to replace, but to co-ordinate the considerable amount of good-neighbourliness which takes place—a matching of needs with offers of help.

At Broxbourne they have in the last year adopted the 'Fish Scheme', and we think this might be the best for us too. (Although the fish is a Christian symbol, the scheme deliberately goes over all boundaries and can involve anyone.)

A preliminary meeting, to give more information, will be held at Pope John Hall, Crossbrook Street on Monday 22 April at 8 p.m.

NB The fish was a secret sign of the early Christians; the initial letters, in Greek, of 'Jesus Christ Son of God Saviour' spell the Greek word for 'fish'.

From a church news letter

256 Death of a Friend

He was fearless in telling the truth to friend and foe. If a man's behaviour was wrong he did not fear saying so. He spoke strongly against people who contributed or listened to idle gossip. He spoke strongly against people who delighted in seeing others in misery. He rebuked the oppressors and comforted the miserable. He mixed freely with the rich and poor, educated and illiterate, white and black. All sections of the people felt he was their man.

From an obituary to Dr William Nkomo by Thomas Nkama

257 Festival

Tanabata-Sama is the Star Festival celebrated by many Chinese and Japanese children. It takes place on the seventh day of the seventh month of the Chinese year. This is because this date commemorates an old legend which tells the tale of a princess who fell in love with a shepherd boy. Both the princess and the shepherd boy lived in the sky and were stars. The girl's father was furious when he heard that she wished to see the shepherd, and he ordered that she should only be allowed to make the journey across the sky to meet the boy once a year.

Children now remember this happy day for the two young stars by decorating trees with paper streamers and lanterns.

258 A Cyrenian Christmas

Billy sat down to his turkey dinner with twenty others in All Saints' Church Hall in Bedford. He crossed himself and then looked around him with tears in his eyes.

'D'ye know,' he said in his soft Irish voice, 'this is the first time I have sat down to a Christmas dinner since I left the family homestead in Donegal more than twenty years back.' The rest of the table joined in with similar remarks.

'It's a damn sight better than a bit of stale pork pie in a cold shed,' said another. 'You can say that again,' rejoined Michael through a mouthful of turkey.

This Christmas dinner had been organised by the Bedford Cyrenian Group as part of their ministry to men and women who sleep rough in the town. The group took over the Church Hall on Christmas Eve until the following Sunday in order to give accommodation and hospitality to people who normally would have to spend the season in allotment sheds and derelict houses. The hall was decorated and furnished with easy chairs, a television set and mattresses for sleeping. Food had been supplied by the generosity of stores and individuals in the town. The hall was staffed by the Cyrenian team under the leadership of Miss Diana Sternfeld and Mr Richard Lomas, the two full time workers.

During the Christmas Season two hundred and thirty eight meals were cooked and served and an average of sixteen slept in the hall each night. The largest number on any one night was twenty five. It was a sad moment when Sunday came round and it was time for the men to go back to their open-air life again.

'Goodbye,' said Billy, shaking hands with the Cyrenian helper. 'Thank you for giving me a real Christmas.'

Denis Desert

259 Go Placidly

Go placidly amid the noise and haste, and remember what peace there may be in silence. As far as possible without surrender be on good terms with all persons. Speak your truth quietly and clearly; and listen to others, even the dull and ignorant; they too have their story.

Avoid loud and aggressive persons, they are vexations to the spirit. If you compare yourself with others, you may become vain and bitter; for always there will be greater and lesser persons than yourself. Enjoy your achievements as well as your plans.

Keep interested in your own career, however humble; it is a real possession in the changing fortunes of time. Exercise caution in your business affairs; for the world is full of trickery. But let this not blind you to what virtue there is; many persons strive for high ideals; and everywhere life is full of heroism.

Be yourself. Especially do not feign affection. Neither be cynical about love; for in the face of all aridity and disenchantment it is perennial as the grass.

Take kindly the counsel of the years, gracefully surrendering the things of youth. Nurture strength of spirit to shield you in sudden misfortune. But do not distress yourself with imaginings. Many fears are born of fatigue and loneliness. Beyond a wholesome discipline, be gentle with yourself.

You are a child of the universe, no less than the trees and the stars; you have a right to be here. And whether or not it is clear to you, no doubt the universe is unfolding as it should.

Therefore be at peace with God, whatever you conceive him to be, and whatever your labours and aspirations, in the noisy confusion of life keep peace with your soul.

Be careful; strive to be happy. With all its sham, drudgery and broken dreams, it is still a beautiful world.

Dated 1692 and found in a church in Baltimore in the United States of America

260 Kindness Out Of Chaos

Would it be possible through your columns to thank most sincerely the taxi driver who gave my fifteen year old son a lift on Monday evening. Because of a bomb scare David was ushered out of Liverpool Street station to complete chaos. There were queues for buses and telephones and he was quite confused.

However a passing taxi stopped and David explained that he had only twenty one pence and wanted to reach Bethnal Green. Not only did the taxi driver accept his story, but then refused to take anything for the journey. A million thanks to him.

K. Ross (Mrs)

A letter to the Evening Standard *28 November 1974*

261 The Magpie

. . . after that—everything had gone wrong. Koira—the dog was old, certainly, but he'd been part of the family for as long as Erkki—had been killed. Vaino had . . . Erkki frowned, he couldn't understand that . . . what had happened to Vaino? . . . then Juhani—he owed his life to Juhani probably and he couldn't understand that either; he and the hired man had always rasped against each other like sandpaper.

When his father shouted and the curtain rose, it was Vaino who should have taken the part of the hero . . . shot the bear, instead of missing . . . dragged his brother from the jaws of death. And even Erkki's vision of presenting his mother with the thick, rich, glossy pelt—that had gone wrong too. The bear's fur was thin and faded by the summer sun and now it was riddled, ruined by shot.

The changed tone of the motorboat engine roused Erkki from his bitter bewilderment and he saw that they were approaching the jetty at Rantala. Lyttinen's boat was already tied up there and the men were carrying Juhani up into the island.

Somebody was running across a field of flax, probably to telephone.

As Pietari Laakso shut off the engine and let the boat cruise in towards the jetty, a magpie rose with a warning rattle from the roof of the boathouse.

'If I had a gun,' chattered Aukusti, pretending to swing a gun at the bird, 'I'd bring down that old black and white varmint!'

It was a queer thing that, it all happened suddenly, like snapping your finger and thumb.

'Nothing's ever just black and white, you little squirt!' yelled Erkki.

Without realising it he had stood up abruptly in the boat and was watching the magpie, seeing, as if for the first time, its green and bronze-greens and purples and blues glinting subtly as the sun took it. 'Can't you see?'

He hadn't meant to say anything like that, the thought hadn't even entered his head. But somehow it had been put into his lips and he knew it was right. He just knew it was right, even though he couldn't have explained. Nothing in life was ever simply black and white. Yet he was as surprised at his own outburst as was Aukusti and for a moment of time the two boys stared at each other, Aukusti open-mouthed and dismayed.

'Why, you're nuts!' Aukusti almost stuttered. 'Dad . . . he says. . . .'

'Look . . .' Erkki began, speaking through clenched teeth. Then he fell silent. What was the use of arguing? Either you could see or you couldn't. Nothing was just black and white. But even he himself, he had to admit, had until only a few moments ago, failed to realise that.

He frowned wryly, still not completely able to fathom things. Yet he felt strangely satisfied, almost light hearted, at the sudden revelation. Then the boat bumped against the jetty and without a word to the Laaksos, he scrambled out.

Alan C. Jenkins

262   Hands

I went to church on Sunday and we talked about our hands. I used one of mine to put a five pence piece into the collection plate. I thought about my hands when I got home and used them to play with.

Julie (aged 6)

263   Thank You

Dear Editor,

I am writing to thank you for some of our teachers giving up so much of their spare time towards making our school what it is in so many ways. First Miss Jowsey is a teacher I should like to thank. She gives up most of her playtimes for music groups of all sorts. Also Miss Jowsey arranges lots of lovely surprises for our class, such as dancing after our Christmas party.

There are other teachers I think we should all be grateful to. Mr Evans and Miss Beale arrange all our sports and matches. Then Mr Thain and Miss Morris should be thanked greatly for arranging all our art work and helping us with it.

Yours sincerely,

Sandra

From a junior school magazine

264   Book Review

A Time to Laugh is a book by Sara and Stephen Corrin. It has all different stories inside. In fact it has thirty stories. I have only read three of them so far but I liked them so much that I wanted to tell you about this book, and I have had it renewed from the library. The best story I have read is 'Mrs Pepperpot buys macaroni'.

Mrs Pepperpot is called Mrs Pepperpot because she is the size of a pepperpot. Her husband buys all the wrong things so she gets in a muddle. I am sure you will like this book if you read it.

From a junior school magazine

265 Memory of Spring

Jason sat down in the comfortable, deep control chair and pressed one of the buttons on the right side of the control panel. Slowly the scene in the large artificial window began to change in response to his finger's pressure on the button. As Jason watched, the trees in the picture seemed to slowly grow leaves and the whole scene changed from grey and dark to a warm, light green.

'I'm glad you've pressed the Spring selector at last,' said Sara coming up behind him.

'Yes, Dad said I could this morning,' replied Jason. 'When it is Spring you want it to look like Spring.'

Sara grunted her approval as she leaned on the back of her twin brother's chair. They always had a special reason for liking Spring because 21 March was their birthday. Tomorrow, 21 March 2040, they would both be eleven.

'Has Grandad said anything to you about the surprise present?' asked Sara.

'Yes, he told me we'd be setting off early tomorrow by computacar. Whatever it is, apparently we are going on a journey to get it.'

'How strange,' said Sara. 'It must be two years since we were off the block.'

'Yes,' answered Jason, getting up from the chair. Walking past the Selecta-View window he came to the observation square and looked out. The view from this, the two hundred and forty ninth floor, was simply cloud banks as usual.

The sudden purring of the mechanical door as their father approached it from the outside made both the children look round.

'Hello there,' said Dad, as he walked in unzipping his space suit. 'Gosh it was busy up on the satellite today. I'm ready for something good.'

'Here's Mum with the meal now,' said Sara as their mother wheeled in the food console from the outer room.

'Hello dear,' said Mrs Rogan, as her husband walked towards her rubbing his hands in anticipation. 'Odour switch on,' she said as a lovely smell of sausages and onions began to fill the air.

Thirty seconds later Mrs Rogan pressed the dispenser button and the five square centimetre packs slid down into the food tray at the bottom of the console.

'Lovely,' said Dad, as he put his into his mouth. 'Now, I hear Grandad is taking you two out tomorrow.'

'Yes,' answered Jason, swallowing the last of his food compact. 'It's a trip for our birthday present.'

'Hmm,' said Dad. 'I'm not too keen on you leaving the block. After all, whatever you want you've only got to go to the right floor and get it. Why doesn't he take you to the holiday floor for a day?'

'Now, now dear,' said Mrs Rogan. 'Let the old man give them his surprise.'

'I suppose you're right,' muttered Dad.

It was early next morning when Grandad called for the children. When the mechanical door opened and he came in the children saw that he was wearing an old twentieth century suit.

'Happy birthday, both of you!' he said, giving them a hug. 'What have you got?'

'Well,' said Sara, 'It's just like we said last week Grandad. We told our friends what we liked, they fed the information into their computors and the best suggestion came out.'

'So I've got some micro books and a video tape recorder . . .' started Jason before he was interrupted by his sister.

'And I've got two electronic living dolls and . . .'

'They all sound lovely,' said Grandad looking at his watch. 'But we must get away.'

'I hope you won't be disappointed in my present,' he said a few minutes later when they were plummeting past the floors in the downward capsule.

When they eventually arrived at ground level Grandad led the way to the computacar bay. Dad had arranged for the car to be waiting for them and they got in and strapped themselves to the seats.

'I never can get used to these things,' muttered Grandad as he pulled the 'inflate skirt' lever. Jason watched with interest as the old man chose the journey pattern and fed it into the computor. He noted that they were going to the perimeter and that the final programme instruction was 'revert to manual'.

Both of these things were unusual. There was so much to do on the blocks that practically no one ever went to the perimeter, and very few people ever drove manually.

'We're off,' said Grandad as the car moved forward after reaching hovering height. The computor took the necessary avoiding action and soon the speedometer had reached the 100 mark. In less than two hours they had reached the perimeter.

'What now?' asked Sara.

'Just a little manual drive first,' said the old man, who could hardly keep the excitement out of his voice.

'We've never been beyond the perimeter before,' said Jason, 'isn't it dangerous?'

'No,' said Grandad. 'They like to say it is on the blocks because of the condition conform treatment. It doesn't work with me because I'm too old, and there is no danger out here.'

'Look,' said Sara, pointing out of the window, 'three d. trees!'

'Not three d. my dear,' said Grandad, 'real.'

'Gosh I never realised there was such a difference between our selectapictures and these things,' said Jason.

They drove on and the children marvelled at some of the things they were seeing for the first time, wild flowers, streams, grass, and not a bit of concrete in sight.

Eventually Grandad stopped the car and they got out.

'We're going to have a picnic,' he said.

'A picnic, what's that?' said Sara.

'Well it's when we sit out in the open air and eat our food.'

'But we haven't got a food console with us,' said Jason.

'This food was made by a very old friend of mine,' answered Grandad, 'who remembered how to make food from the old days.'

Quietly they sat and ate the strange but wonderful objects which Grandad gave them. 'Sandwiches,' he called most of them. Then they ran about and felt all the things which they had previously only seen pictures of.

Eventually it was time to go. The evening sun provided a red background to the silhouettes of trees and the distant hills.

Jason and Sara could never remember a stranger but more exciting birthday. Sara looked at Grandad who was standing looking at the sunset. Going over to the old man she put her arm through his.

'Thank you,' she said. 'It's been a marvellous day.'

Stan Hodgson

266   Educating Deaf Children

Deaf children can't hear the sound of talking, so they can't learn naturally to understand what words mean or how to use them. Can you remember how you learnt to talk? It would be very hard to learn if you couldn't copy your parents voices, or hear your own voice.

To help them understand words deaf children are taught to lip-read. This means seeing what words look like when they are said. It's hard to do, and some never become good at it. Can you imagine having to lip-read an entire history lesson?

Most deaf children go to special schools where a lot of their time has to be given to learning to lip-read. This means there is not so much time for ordinary lessons. Many words look alike on the lips even though they sound quite different.

Deaf children can also be taught to speak but this is even harder than lip-reading because they cannot hear their own voices. The teacher makes them feel her throat muscles moving and the breath coming out of her mouth. The deaf children copy her and so make sounds we can hear but they never can.

Some partly deaf children if they have a good hearing aid can go to an ordinary school like yours. But for some lessons, especially speech and lip-reading, they might have to have a special teacher.

Hearing aids are worn by deaf children to help them hear sounds more loudly, but they still don't hear as well as you do.

From a leaflet issued by the Royal National Institute for the Deaf

267 Actions or Words?

A farmer lived on a farm with his two boys.

'Tom,' he said to the first boy, 'give me a hand on the farm today.'

'All right, Dad,' he said.

But he didn't go.

The farmer said exactly the same to his second boy, Bill.

'Not I!' said Bill.

But later on he changed his mind, and went to give his father a hand on the farm.

Did Tom, or Bill do what his father wanted?

Matthew XXI 28–31

268

Meanwhile Peter was sitting outside in the courtyard when a serving-maid accosted him and said, 'You were there too with Jesus the Galilean.' Peter denied it in face of them all. 'I do not know what you mean,' he said. He then went out to the gateway, where another girl, seeing him, said to the people there, 'This fellow was with Jesus of Nazareth.' Once again he denied it, saying with an oath, 'I do not know the man.' Shortly afterwards the bystanders came up and said to Peter, 'Surely you are another of them; your accent gives you away!' At this be broke into curses and declared with an oath: 'I do not know the man.' At that moment a cock crew; and Peter remembered how Jesus had said, 'Before the cock crows you will disown me three times.' He went outside, and wept bitterly.

Matthew XXVI 69–75

269

Again he said: 'There was once a man who had two sons; and the younger said to his father, "Father, give me my share of the property." So he divided his estate between them. A few days later the younger son turned the whole of his share into cash and left home for a distant country, where he squandered it in reckless living. He had spent it all, when a severe famine fell upon that country and he began to feel the pinch. So he went and attached himself to one of the local landowners, who sent him on to his farm to mind the pigs. He would have been glad to fill his belly with the pods that the pigs were eating; and no one gave him anything. Then he came to his senses and said, "How many of my father's paid servants have more food than they can eat, and here am I, starving to death! I will set off and go to my father, and say to him, 'Father, I have sinned, against God and against you; I am no longer fit to be called your son; treat me as one of your paid servants.' " So he set out for his father's house. But while he was still a long way off his father saw him, and his heart went out to him. He ran to meet him, flung his arms around him, and kissed him. The son said, "Father, I have sinned, against God and against you; I am no longer fit to be called your son." But the father said to his servants, "Quick! fetch a robe, my best one, and put it on him; put a ring on his finger and shoes on his feet. Bring the fatted calf and kill it, and let us have a feast to celebrate the day. For this son of mine was dead and has come back to life; he was lost and is found." And the festivities began.

'Now the elder son was out on the farm; and on his way back, as he approached the house, he heard music and dancing. He called one of the servants and asked what it meant. The servant told him, "Your brother has come home, and your father has killed the fatted calf because he has him back safe and sound." But he was angry and refused to go in. His father came out and pleaded with him; but he retorted, "You know how I have slaved for you all these years; I have never once disobeyed your orders; and you never gave me so much as a kid, for a feast with my friends. But now that this son of yours turns up, after running through your money with his women, you kill the fatted calf for him.'' ''My boy,'' said the father, ''you are always with me, and everything I have is yours. How could we help celebrating this happy day? Your brother here was dead and has come back to life, was lost, and is found.'' '

Luke XV 11–32

270

When the rats disappeared the mayor was delighted. Soon the Pied Piper came to see him and the town council.

'Can I have the 1000 guilders you promised me?' asked the Piper.

'What 1000 guilders?' replied the mayor. 'We'll give you a hundred.' As he said this he turned to smile at the town council as if to say, 'This fellow has got rid of the rats. What can he do if we only pay him a tenth of our promise?'

'People of honour always keep their promises and bargains,' said the Piper quickly.

'Are you threatening me?' asked the mayor with a lot of huffing and puffing. 'Be off with you.'

The Piper looked around him with a sad and disappointed look on his face. Then . . . he lifted his pipe again.

From The Pied Piper of Hamelin

271 Knowing Your Own Mind

One day a miller and his son got ready to go to market. They were going to sell their donkey.

'If we keep him fresh we'll get more money for him,' said the son.

'Righto,' said the miller. 'Come on, we'll tie his feet together and hang him from this pole. If we each have one end of the pole on our shoulders he'll have a restful ride.'

They did this and set out. They hadn't got very far before they met another traveller.

'You must be mad!' he said. 'Fancy carrying a donkey!'

The miller and his son looked worriedly at each other.

'Perhaps he's right,' said the miller. 'Put him down, and then you ride him.'

Off they went again with the miller walking in front and his son riding the donkey. Soon they came across another traveller.

'You idle fellow,' he shouted, 'get down and let your father ride.'

Both the miller and his son were very worried about this comment so they changed places. No sooner had they done so than a man passing in the other direction called out to them.

'Lazy old man, why don't you let your son ride for a change?'

'There's only one thing left,' said the miller. 'Get up beside me.'

So the miller's son climbed up beside his father, and the donkey walked on much more slowly with its heavy load. When they reached the town where the market was held people turned to stare at them and then began to hiss and boo.

'Cruelty! Look at that poor animal. Get off and walk you two!'

The miller stopped the donkey and he and his son dismounted. Looking at his son the miller said, 'Well I've certainly learned something on this journey!'

Adapted from La Fontaine

272 Hallowe'en Traditions

Duck-apple and Snap-apple are two popular games which are
played at Hallowe'en. In the first game the apples are floated in
a large bowl of water. The children who are playing the game
then gather round the bowl. First they are blindfolded and then
they have their hands tied behind their backs. Then they have
to try and take a bite out of one of the floating apples. Of
course they can't see, they can't use their hands and they are
not allowed to wedge an apple against the side of the bowl
either!

In Snap-apple the apple is tied onto a piece of string and then
dangles from the roof, just within reach of the contestants'
mouths. Again the idea is to try and take a bite from the apple,
and again it is forbidden for hands to be used to steady the
apple.

These games have been played by children for hundreds of
years. They first came into being however when people
celebrated the end of gathering in the fruit. Like the last sheaf
of corn at the harvest, people felt that they must 'honour' the
fruit and show their thankfulness for having been provided
with fruit for the winter.

Anon

273 Justice?

The room in which the boys were fed, was a large stone hall,
with a copper at one end: out of which the master, dressed in
an apron for the purpose, and assisted by one or two women,
ladled the gruel at meal-times. Of this festive composition each
boy had one porringer, and no more—except on occasions of
great public rejoicing, when he had two ounces and a quarter
of bread besides. The bowls never wanted washing. The boys
polished them with their spoons till they shone again; and
when they had performed this operation (which never took
very long, the spoons being nearly as large as the bowls), they

would sit staring at the copper, with such eager eyes, as if they could have devoured the very bricks of which it was composed; employing themselves, meanwhile, in sucking their fingers most assiduously, with the view of catching up any stray splashes of gruel that might have been cast thereon. Boys have generally excellent appetites. Oliver Twist and his companions suffered the tortures of slow starvation for three months; at last they got so voracious and wild with hunger, that one boy, who was tall for his age, and hadn't been used to that sort of thing (for his father had kept a small cook-shop), hinted darkly to his companions, that unless he had another basin of gruel per diem, he was afraid he might some night happen to eat the boy who slept next him, who happened to be a weakly youth of tender age. He had a wild, hungry eye; and they implicitly believed him. A council was held; lots were cast who should walk up to the master after supper that evening, and ask for more; and it fell to Oliver Twist.

The evening arrived; the boys took their places. The master, in his cook's uniform, stationed himself at the copper; his pauper assistants ranged themselves behind him; the gruel was served out; and a long grace was said over the short commons. The gruel disappeared; the boys whispered to each other, and winked at Oliver; while his next neighbours nudged him. Child as he was, he was desperate with hunger, and reckless with misery. He rose from the table; and advancing to the master, basin and spoon in hand, said: somewhat alarmed at his own temerity:

'Please, Sir, I want some more.'

The master was a fat, healthy man; but he turned very pale. He gazed in stupefied astonishment on the small rebel for some seconds, and then clung for support to the copper. The assistants were paralysed with wonder; the boys with fear.

'What!' said the master at length, in a faint voice.

'Please, Sir,' replied Oliver, 'I want some more.'

The master aimed a blow at Oliver's head with the ladle; pinioned him in his arms; and shrieked aloud for the beadle.

The board were sitting in solemn conclave, when Mr Bumble rushed into the room in great excitement, and addressing the gentleman in the high chair, said,

'Mr Limbkins, I beg your pardon, Sir! Oliver Twist has asked for more!'

There was a general start. Horror was depicted on every countenance.

'For more!' said Mr Limbkins. 'Compose yourself, Bumble, and answer me distinctly. Do I understand that he asked for more, after he had eaten the supper allotted by the dietary?'

'He did, Sir,' replied Bumble.

'That boy will be hung,' said the gentleman in the white waistcoat. 'I know that boy will be hung.'

From Oliver Twist *by Charles Dickens*

274 Equality

For three months after that night Mowgli hardly ever left the village gate, he was so busy learning the ways and customs of men. First he had to wear a cloth round him, which annoyed him horribly; and then he had to learn about money, which he did not in the least understand, and about ploughing, of which he did not see the use. Then the little children in the village made him very angry. Luckily, the Law of the Jungle had taught him to keep his temper, for the Jungle life and food depend on keeping your temper; but when they made fun of him because he would not play games or fly kites, or because he mispronounced some word, only the knowledge that it was unsportsmanlike to kill little naked cubs kept him from picking them up and breaking them in two.

He did not know his own strength in the least. In the Jungle he knew he was weak compared with the beasts, but in the village people said that he was as strong as a bull.

And Mowgli had not the faintest idea of the difference that caste makes between man and man. When the potter's donkey slipped in the clay-pit, Mowgli hauled it out by the tail, and helped to stack the pots for their journey to the market at Khaniwara. That was very shocking, too, for the potter is a low-caste man, and his donkey is worse.

From The Jungle Book *by Rudyard Kipling*

275   Good Times

. . . when father got home—a little early because he had invited them all to drive as a part of Jane's birthday present—they were ready for him, washed and brushed as he liked them to be. Only Hubert was a little behind. He had scratched an old mosquito bite and it wouldn't stop bleeding. Nurse had cuffed him for it, but not before the top of his white sock was spoiled, and then he couldn't find another pair. 'Never mind,' said Father, 'tell him to put on brown ones.' He was in such a good humour they came rushing downstairs forgetting to be quiet any longer.

Driving like this, with the pair of horses, and the back-board of the democrat wagon down, was one of the things they liked best to do. There were turns for who should sit in front and Father was quite fair about it. Even in the back there was no end to the privileges they had today because it was Jane's birthday. While the white dust steamed up on either side, slightly warmed and smelling of the stables, and while they watched the way it settled cloudlike at the farther end of the road, they swung their legs in a quick even time to the trot, trot, trot of the horses. Jane had brought a stick and she let one end scrape along behind so that it made a fine clear wiggling mark on the plain surface of the road and sent up spurts and showers of dirt when she pressed it down with both hands. Sometimes she let it hop loosely and then it bounced from the tops of stones and uneven places. Hubert asked to try and she gave it to him. He used it to lay against one of the wheels and make a fountain of earth fly out.

When it was Jane's turn to sit in front she was allowed to touch the horses lightly now and then with the whip and feel them answer instantly to this infinitesimal flick of the lash, and when it was Theodore's turn to sit at the back he had brought with him two pocketfuls of stones and they flung them at the passing trees. Occasionally Father let the horses out which meant that they flew and saw the country only as a sea of melted green.

On the way home they settled themselves into limp attitudes of content. Jane lay back along the length of the carriage and watched the white radiant blobs of cloud. Theodore took her stick and made it jump tremendously. Hubert, in front, let the whip down at one side and caught the tongue around a daisy head. Father only calmly told him not to. Jane wished it could be like this forever.

From A Lemon and a Star *by E. C. Spykman*

276   An Enchanted Garden

I shall never forget my surprise and delight on first beholding the bottom of the sea . . . The water within the reef was as calm as a pond; and, as there was no wind, it was quite clear, from the surface to the bottom, so that we could see down easily even at a depth of twenty or thirty yards. When Jack and I dived into shallower water, we expected to have found sand and stones, instead of which we found ourselves in what appeared really to be an enchanted garden. The whole of the bottom of the lagoon, as we called the calm water within the reef, was covered with coral of every shape, size and hue. Some portions were formed like large mushrooms; others appeared like the brain of a man, having stalks or necks attached to them; but the most common kind was a species of branching coral, and some portions were of a lovely pale, pink colour, others were pure white. Among this there grew large quantities

216

of seaweed of the richest hues imaginable, and of the most graceful forms; while innumerable fishes—blue, red, yellow, green and striped—sported in and out among the flower beds of this submarine garden.

From The Coral Island *by R. M. Ballantyne*

277   'Necessities?'

People living in highly developed countries assume that the following 'necessities' of life will be readily available in sufficient quantity or of an adequate quality:
shelter and sanitation
food and clothing
transport facilities
employment and an adequate income
education
health facilities.

There are people in Britain who are deprived of one or more of these 'necessities'. Nonetheless, these 'fundamental rights' are the accepted norms of our society.

Thereafter, depending upon income and life-style, certain 'luxuries' will be considered 'essential':
an attractive environment
adequate furnishings and household articles, selected more for appearance than utility
individual transport facilities (cars, bikes etc.)
leisure facilities (both public and private)
individual personal possessions (such as children's toys)
an adequate selection of alternative clothing
books, newspapers and television.

From a Save the Children pamphlet

278 The Way to the Well

There was once a farmer in Spain who had three sons and a daughter. One day the farmer became very ill and a passing traveller told his family that he could only be saved by the water of life.

'Where do we get that from?' said Alonso, the eldest son.

'From a well on a mountain top which is three days hard riding away from here,' said the stranger.

So Alonso set off. After three days riding he came to the mountain. An old man sat at the bottom of it.

'I suppose you've come for some of the water of life,' said the old man.

'Yes, I have,' said Alonso.

'Well you get it from a well up there,' said the old man, nodding towards the mountain top. 'But let me give you some advice. As you climb you will find that many of the stones shout and jeer and mock you. Don't look at them or touch them whatever you do.'

'Hmm,' thought Alonso, 'that sounds ridiculously easy.'

He began climbing the mountain. Immediately stones began to jeer at him and call him names. He paid no attention until one in particular began to shout: 'You're a boaster Alonso, always bragging and boasting.'

When he heard this Alonso was furious, perhaps because this insult was rather near the truth. Angrily he turned towards the stone and . . . immediately turned into a stone himself.

Two weeks later the second son Carlo set out, to get the water of life, and to find his brother. He found the mountain, and the old man, and received exactly the same warning.

Soon he was climbing up the mountain. He ignored the cries of the stones . . . until suddenly he thought he heard his brother's voice. He looked to see where it was coming from . . . and was immediately turned into a stone.

A week later the third son, Alfredo, was on the mountain. Having heard the old man's warning he was singing and whistling to drown the sounds of the stones's voices. Suddenly he tripped, and as he fell he thought he heard a voice he recognised. He turned to look . . . and was turned into a stone.

The old farmer was by now very weak and in a last desperate effort to save his life Maria, his daughter, set off to find the water of life. When she had heard the old man of the mountain's warning she set off up the path her brothers had already taken.

Now Maria knew that her father's life depended on her getting the water, so no matter what the stones shouted she kept her eyes fixed on the well up ahead. Eventually she reached it and filled her goatskin full of the precious liquid. As she did so a drop fell on a stone nearby, and immediately it turned into a man.

At once Maria felt she must help here too, and at that moment the cries of the stones all stopped. Sprinkling a drop on each large stone Maria began to move slowly down the mountain. Behind her there gathered an ever increasing crowd of men and women, including her brothers.

Finally she reached the bottom, with just enough of the water of life to take home to her father. With the whole crowd cheering and thanking her, Maria and her brothers set off for home. When they arrived it needed only a few drops of the water to restore her father to good health.

Adapted from an old Spanish legend

279 'I'm Staying!'

'It's going to be a tricky one,' said Lieutenant John Mould of the Royal Australian Navy as he looked out across the long stretch of mud and sand.

What he was looking at appeared to be a very large tin barrel lying in the mud of Trinity Sands at the mouth of the River Humber in Yorkshire. John Mould knew however that this thing which looked like a barrel was in fact a new and highly dangerous mine, which could explode at any minute. As a member of the 'Rendering Mines Safe' squad it was John's job to try and stop the mine exploding and killing people.

'We're going to have to hurry,' said Lieutenant Geoffrey Turner, who stood beside Mould. 'We'll have to get out there while the tide is out, de-fuse the mine, and then get back before we are cut off by the tide coming in.'

'Not we . . . I,' said Lieutenant Mould. 'Remember you're just here to learn the job. That mine looks a new kind to me. Far too dangerous for you to start learning on.'

Lieutenant Turner didn't answer but when John Mould began to take careful steps through the mud towards the sand, he followed. Mould didn't say anything. He was too busy watching the mine.

After about ten minutes the two men reached the dangerous weapon. When Mould looked closely at it he felt both relieved and worried. He was relieved because he could see that the parts he had to get to, which were the primer and the detonator, were not buried in the mud. He was worried because he could see that it was a new acoustic mine.

This meant that it could be exploded by any fairly steady noise. The vibrations of such a noise would set off the mine's mechanism and both he and Turner would be killed instantly. To make it safe he had to unscrew the keeper-ring and then pull out the spring which held the detonator in place.

Whilst a sudden sharp noise might not set off the mine any rattling of tools almost certainly would. He turned to Turner and whispered, 'Buzz off now.'

Lieutenant Turner shook his head, put his finger to his lips and then pointed to the bag of tools which he had carefully laid on the mud between them. He mimed getting out a tool and handing it to Mould.

Lieutenant Mould nodded in relief. He knew that if Geoffrey Turner stayed, took out the tools one at a time and gave them silently to him it would make what appeared to be almost an impossible job both quicker and safer. He also knew that the slightest mistake on his part would kill not only himself but Turner as well.

He turned to see Lieutenant Turner holding out a wrench to him. As he took it the other man gave a broad grin and winked. Now Mould gave all his concentration to the job in hand.

Turning the keeper-ring with agonising slowness Lieutenant Mould began to ease it off. When it was almost ready to come off he handed the tool back to Turner and held it with his hand. Then as he eased it off he put his other hand underneath it to hold the spring still in place. He was frightened that if he let the spring jump out it would rattle on the casing and set off the mine.

Ever so slowly he began to lift the keeper-ring away from the mine. When it was off he laid it on the mud and began to let the pressure of the spring ease up into his hand. When he felt that it was free, he pulled quickly and it was out!

Sweat poured down the faces of both men as they knelt there knowing that if the mine was activated there was nothing that they could do now. Seconds passed and nothing happened. Lieutenant Mould turned to Geoffrey Turner and put out his hand. Muddy and exhausted the two men shook hands. There was no need for words. This was one mine which wasn't going to go off now.

Geoffrey Simpson

280 Report from Jerusalem

There has been great excitement in this famous city over the past few days. It began with the arrival of the man everybody is talking about in these parts. His name is Jesus Christ. Although just a carpenter's son this man has built up a great reputation in a very short time and there are many people who will tell of his sensational powers. The other day Jesus Christ arrived at the gates of the city, riding on an ass.

Never in my years of reporting have I seen anything like it. There was a tremendous crowd to greet him, and his welcome was like that of a popular hero. He showed something of his personal charm too. Within a short time of entering the city he had befriended one of the most unpopular men here, a notorious tax collector.

Since that momentous first appearance the city has been full of rumours, sensational events and intrigue, all of which seem to surround Jesus Christ. There was a violent scene in the temple when he was quick to anger at the sight of the customary market place activities.

Wherever he goes in the city there are crowds and excitement and a feeling that unusual things are going to happen. The government have remained very quiet during all this activity. I have it on good authority however that the members of the Sanhedrin consider this man a trouble maker, a disturber of the peace and a revolutionary. There are rumours that spies are collecting information about Christ's deeds and that he will soon be arrested.

Also it seems . . . excuse me here is a news flash . . . and it is very important!

Apparently there was a plot to make sure that Jesus Christ was arrested. Tonight he was having a meal with a group of his special friends. During the meal one of these so called friends left the group and went to see the members of the Sanhedrin. It is said that he provided them with 'helpful information' and will receive a reward for his services. The name of this man has been released. It is Judas Iscariot.

Geoffrey Simpson

281   Thrills at the Track

Eliott kept his eye on the starter's flag. The powerful car purred, ready to roar into action as soon as he pressed his foot on the accelerator. Around him he could see the helmets and goggles of the other drivers as they sat, like him, waiting for the race to start.

Suddenly the flag dropped and, like a charge of mechanical monsters, the racing cars leapt forward with a tremendous roar. Eliott kept his eyes to the front but he was aware of blue and red cars slipping past him as he sped into the lead, and the first bend.

The screech of tyres mixed with the smell of burning rubber as he flung his car into the bend. With an expert twist of the steering wheel he was round and then speeding away into the long flat straight. Behind him the other cars fought for a good position as they rounded the corner. Eliott wasn't bothered about them. Ahead of him the road was empty and flashing by beneath his tyres at more than one hundred miles an hour. He was in the lead!

For lap after lap Eliott held his position. As he swung past the pits to begin his final circuit he saw by the 'thumbs up' signs from his mechanics that he was still well in front. All he had to do was drive carefully for a few minutes and he would be certain to win.

Again the starting bend came, and threading his way past three cars who were several laps behind him Eliott pressed his foot hard to the floor as he began his last run down the long straight. Suddenly he was aware that the powerful thrust of the engine was fading. He pressed his foot harder on the accelerator. Something was wrong! The great car was slowing down. The engine had stopped.

Eliott felt a terrible sense of disappointment as thoughts flashed through his mind. After leading all the way he was going to lose the race. But, he thought as the car began to glide more slowly, I'll certainly finish it. Checking that he was in no danger from passing cars Eliott released his seat belt and jumped out. Before the car had a chance to stop he began pushing it.

Using all his strength he was able to keep it moving as he ran alongside. Cars began to pass him rapidly now and he knew that the leaders would soon be overtaking him. As he ran along the last half mile of the 'straight' he was aware of a tremendous noise. Then he realised what it was. The people in the grandstands were standing up and cheering.

As he saw the chequered flag get nearer the cheering and clapping got louder. Despite the blisters on his feet and hands, and the pain in his chest as he gasped for breath, Eliott suddenly no longer felt disappointed.

He'd lost the race but at this moment that somehow didn't seem so important.

Geoffrey Simpson

282   Lost and Found

Silas Grant owned a shop. It sold newspapers, magazines, comics, sweets, cigarettes, ice cream and in fact almost anything you could think of!

Silas however was one of those people who was always grumbling. He hated getting up early in the morning so when his delivery boy came to collect the papers to give out he often had to wait around. This meant that he would be late for school, so he gave up his job. So did the next boy, and the next.

'No good, any of 'em,' grumbled Silas as more and more customers cancelled their orders because they didn't get their morning paper before they went to work. As he couldn't be bothered to keep his shelves properly organised sometimes when customers came in Silas couldn't find what they wanted. These people didn't come back to his shop.

One day Silas heard that the streets round about his shop were going to be pulled down.

'It's all right though.' said the man who was telling him this, 'they're going to build some very pleasant flats and maisonettes here. It will be much better then. People'll be a lot more comfortable than they have been in these old houses.'

'Huh it's all right for you,' moaned Silas, 'but what about me? After all the work I've put in keeping my shop. After all I've done for the people in this neighbourhood. Now they'll all be clearing out I suppose. Never give me a thought. Typical!'

Silas's customer looked at the grumbling shopkeeper with a doubtful look in his eye. When he was having his tea later in the day he mentioned the conversation to his wife.

'What an old misery that man is,' said his wife. 'Listen Albert, why don't we make him an offer for his shop? You know you can't do any more work as a steeplejack after you were hurt in that fall. We've got enough money for a deposit.'

The next day Silas heard the bell of his shop door click. It didn't ring because it had been broken for weeks and he couldn't be bothered to fix it. He saw his customer was Albert Gardener again.

'Miserable out there today,' grunted Silas as he wiped his hands on his dirty overall and leaned against the counter. 'Well what can I do for you?'

'It's like this Silas,' said Albert and then he put his proposition to the dissatisfied shopkeeper.

About an hour later the two men shook hands on the deal.

Albert wondered if he'd done the right thing but he thought that with hard work he could make the shop into a good one.

As soon as Albert had gone out Silas rubbed his hands together. 'What a mug,' he muttered to himself. 'Fancy buying this dump. All the customers moving away. Still I should have squeezed a bit more out of him.'

A year later great changes had taken place in the lives of both men. Albert and his wife were living in the flat above the shop. It had been a year of very hard work. First Albert had painted the outside of the shop. Then at nights he had set out the shelves so that he knew exactly where everything was. He'd got up very early each morning and delivered the papers himself so that he was sure the customers would get them.

Word that he was a pleasant, helpful man had begun to spread around however. He now had a paper boy working for him. As well as that the new flats were beginning to fill up and lots more people were coming into his shop. Many of them were strangers to the area and a friendly smile and a few words made them feel more at home. Yes it had been a hard year thought Albert, but it was worth every minute of it. He'd tried his best and he thought people appreciated that.

Meanwhile Silas had taken the money he had got for the shop and bought a beautiful little bungalow at the seaside. But when a fence had blown down in the winter he couldn't be bothered to put it up, and he was always complaining to his neighbours that there were no shops nearby and that everything was more expensive here at the seaside.

As he was always grumbling his neighbours were inclined to keep out of his way. So Silas hadn't made any friends and he was thinking of moving on again.

'Rotten dump here,' he thought as he stuck a piece of cardboard over a window pane he had broken when trying to force a stiff window open.

Stan Hodgson

283　Primitive Beliefs

In the fifteenth century a group of people called Aztecs lived in Mexico. They worshipped a god they thought of as the Sun God. In order to have this god look favourably on them they thought it was necessary to please him by building huge temples. They also felt that he would be even more pleased if they offered him human sacrifice as well. Consequently when the great temple to the Sun God was finished in Mexico in the year 1487 thousands of people had their hearts cut out as a human sacrifice for this occasion.

284　Statistics

World War I (1914–1918)—8 500 000 soldiers killed.
World War II (1939–1945)—6 000 000 Jews killed in concentration camps.
World War II (1939–1945)—135 000 people killed in Dresden air raids by British and American bombers.

285　To the Leader of an Alien Planet Who is Rumoured to be About to Attack Earth

Dear Leader,

I don't think it would be very wise to go to war with Earth because we have things that could be of use to you, and perhaps we could exchange for something of yours. I think this would be much simpler because no-one would get hurt. Perhaps we could meet to talk about these things.

Yours sincerely,

Simon

Schoolboy (aged 10)

286

Dear Sir,

I like reading newspapers and watching television but have
you ever thought about all the good news in the world. Too
often we read about, and see bad news. Couldn't we hear more
about the good news?

Yours sincerely,

'Hertfordshire Area' (aged ten)

287

One of the things we always want to protest about is the rubbish that is spread about our town. We've got rubbish bins but nobody seems to use them. There is litter all over the streets, and loads of it thrown in the river. As well as that there is too much broken glass around in parks which might be a danger to small children and animals.

We would like to start a club for clearing up our town, and other towns and cities.

Nigel and David (both aged 11)

288   Joy

I heard the door open but I didn't know who had come in. Then I heard a dog whine and I knew it must be my family and our collie Bruce. I heard the kind voice of the matron saying, 'It's all right dear, we're just going to take the bandage off your eyes, that's all.'

My heart missed a beat with excitement. I felt matron's hands unwrapping the bandage. The first thing I saw was the light creeping in from under the blinds. I squinted at it. Then I saw Bruce looking at me, and he licked my face.

Mum and Dad smiled at me and sister Sue gave me a present. I looked round my room. Never had I seen such a lovely room, and I had been in it for five days and this was the first time I had seen it.

Betty (aged 10)

289   Cruelty

I am interested in dogs and I am horrified at some of the things adults do with their so-called pets. For instance here are three of them. I saw on television about how a man had taught his ɑog to smoke a pipe. This just seems stupid and a waste of time.

Worse than that I read in a book at school where a man in Ireland had been stopped for letting his dog drive his car! He said it could steer with its front legs and change gear with its back legs and he taught it to do this because his own licence was suspended. This is foolish and and dangerous.

Worst of all though is the story about the dog in the swimming pool next to my sister's school. One night people who live near there heard some terrible yelping and when they came to find out what was happening they found that someone had thrown a dog into the school swimming pool. As the sides are high the dog couldn't get out and it was drowning. How can people be so cruel?

James (aged 12)

290   Hero

A part-time paratrooper who saved the life of a comrade whose parachute failed to open by wrapping his legs round the other's rigging lines, has been awarded the Queen's Gallantry Medal.

CSM John McRae, aged thirty eight, of Fifteen (Volunteer Scottish Battalion) Parachute Regiment is the first TAVR soldier to win the medal which was instituted in June. The incident happened during a weekend exercise last summer.

From The Guardian *26 November 1974*

291   Quasimodo

We shall not attempt to give the reader any idea of that horse-shoe mouth, of that little left eye, stubbled up with an eyebrow of carroty bristles, while the right was completely overwhelmed and buried by an enormous wen; of those irregular teeth, jagged here and there like the battlements of a fortress; of that horny lip, over which one of those teeth protruded, like the tusk of an elephant; of that forked chin; and above all, of the expression, the mixture of spite, wonder and melancholy, spread over these exquisite features. Imagine such an object, if you can. . . .

. . . His prodigious head was covered with red bristles; between his shoulders rose an enormous hump, which was counterbalanced by a protuberance in front; his thighs and legs were so strangely put together that they touched at no one point but the knees, and seen in front, resembled two sickles joined at the handles; his feet were immense, his hands monstrous; but, with all this deformity, there was a formidable air of strength, agility and courage. . . . He looked like a giant who had been broken in pieces and ill soldered together.

From The Hunchback of Notre Dame *by Victor Hugo*

292   Shadows

When they dropped the atom bomb there was a terrible explosion and a terrifically strong blast. People were blown against trees and buildings. When it was over only shadows were left in the slight breeze.

Adapted from some comments by a twelve-year-old boy

293   Medal for Bomb Hero

An army major who risked his life to defuse a wartime bomb, a fireman who rescued three people from a burning guest house, and two teenagers who foiled an Ulster terrorist bombing receive awards today for their courage.

Major Arthur Hogben, stationed at Rochester, Kent, receives the Queen's Gallantry Medal for dealing with Hermann, the 2200 pound bomb discovered in Plaistow, East London, in August.

When the bomb was found, 1000 people were evacuated from

their homes. Major Hogben used steam on the heat-sensitive device to remove nearly a ton of high explosive.

Leading Fireman John Colley, of the Devon fire brigade, rescued a man and a woman from the burning building as flames spread through the top floor. Then, without the aid of breathing apparatus, he battled through the thick smoke again to a third unconscious person.

But he was forced back by the heat. Firemen with breathing equipment were unable to get through the narrow window, So Mr Colley again fought through the smoke and dragged the victim clear.

He receives the George Medal for his courage.

Paul Partington and Lindsay Lockhart, both aged sixteen, risked their lives when they realised a terrorist bomb was due to go off in a crowded building in Northern Ireland.

They dashed inside to raise the alarm, and everyone inside escaped the blast. The boys—whose addresses are being kept secret for security reasons—receive the Queen's Commendation.

The Queen's Gallantry Medal is awarded to three policemen who chased and arrested a man during a running gun battle. They are Constables Godfrey Chaffey, Barry Gage, and Alan Pointer of the Metropolitan Police.

Constables Gage and Chaffey chased a man seen running from a restaurant with the proprietor's wife's handbag. As the man drove off in a car, he fired several shots but the constables were not hit. Constable Pointer gave chase in a police van and disarmed the gunman when he crashed his car and attempted to fire at the officer. The gunman and accomplice were arrested after a violent struggle.

An RAF fighter pilot, who landed his crippled aircraft at a strange base after a hundred-mile struggle to maintain height, is awarded the Queen's Commendation for Valuable Services in the Air.

Flight-Lieutenant Nigel James Day, serving on his first operational tour with Number Forty Five Squadron at RAF Wittering, near Peterborough, was flying in bad weather over the North Sea during a NATO exercise when the engine of his Hunter virtually failed.

From The Guardian *17 December 1974*

294 The Meeting

My life with Anna began on such a night. I was nineteen at the time, prowling the streets and alleys with my usual supply of hot dogs, the street lights with their foggy haloes showing dark formless shapes moving out from the darkness of the fog and disappearing again. Down the street a little way a baker's shop window softened and warmed the raw night with its gas lamps. Sitting on the grating under the window was a little girl. In those days children wandering the streets at night were no uncommon sight. I had seen such things before, but on this occasion it was different. How or why it was different has long since been forgotten except that I am sure it was different. I sat down beside her on the grating, my back against the shop front. We stayed there about three hours. Looking back over thirty years, I can now cope with those three hours; but at the time I was on the verge of being destroyed. That November night was pure hell; my guts tied themselves into all manner of complicated knots.

Perhaps even then something of her angelic nature caught hold of me; I'm quite prepared to believe that I had been bewitched from the beginning. I sat down with 'Shove up a bit, Tich.' She shoved up a bit but made no comment.

'Have a hot dog,' I said.

She shook her head and answered, 'It's yours.'

'I got plenty. Besides, I'm full up,' I said.

She made no sign so I put the bag on the grating between us. The light from the shop window wasn't very strong and the kid was sitting in the shadows so I couldn't see what she looked like except that she was very dirty. I could see that she clutched under one arm a rag-doll and on her lap a battered old paint-box.

We sat there for thirty minutes or so in a complete silence; during that time I thought there had been a movement of her hand towards the hot dog bag but I didn't want to look or comment in case I put her off. Even now I can feel the immense pleasure I had when I heard the sound of that hot dog skin popping under the bite of her teeth. A minute of two later she took a second and then a third. I reached into my pocket and brought out a packet of Woodbines.

'Do you mind if I smoke while you're eating, Tich?' I asked.

'What?' She sounded a little alarmed.

'Can I have a fag while you're eating?'

She rolled over and got to her knees and looked me in the face.

'Why?' she said.

'My mum's a stickler for politeness. Besides, you don't blow smoke in a lady's face when she's eating,' I said.

She stared at half a sausage for a moment or two, and looking at me fully, she said, 'Why? Do you like me?'

I nodded.

'You have a fag then,' and she smiled at me and popped the rest of the sausage into her mouth.

I took out a Woodbine and lit up and offered her the match to blow out. She blew, and I was sprayed with bits of sausage. This little accident produced such a reaction in her that I felt that I had been stabbed in the guts. I had seen a dog cringe before, but never a child. The look she gave me was filled with horror. She expected a thrashing. She clenched her teeth as she waited for me to strike her.

From Mister God this is Anna *by Fynn*

295   The Joy of Dancing

The joy of dancing is the exhilarating feeling of moving to well played music, which makes our blood tingle and our feet tap the floor, and urges us to respond by moving in rhythm.

Dancing brings boys and girls together in a unique way. It helps to makes friends. There is no language barrier—in fact, dancing is an international language in itself.

Frank and Peggy Spicer writing in The Project Club—Project Manual

296   An Old Lady I Know

This old lady used to be the bank cleaner and we got very friendly with her. Her real name is Mrs W . . . but we call her Weddy. She is ninety two just after Christmas, but even though she's very old she still can have a bit of fun and she's very rarely sad.

Weddy's fingers have grown so much that she has no nails because her fingers have overlapped them.

Her face is wizened and wrinkled and she's nearly deaf, her mouth is a round shape like an 'O' and when she's finished speaking her mouth seems to twitch.

She cannot walk properly and she hobbles and she's never without an old umbrella which she walks with.

Her hair is dark grey and she wears it in a bun on the back of her head.

She lives by herself in a little cottage in S . . . Lane.

One day Weddy came to our house to visit us and all the time she was there she kept her hat on even though she took her coat off. She wears very long clothes, mostly black. When she went from our house she had to go down the stairs and it nearly took her all day because she went down one at a time and my daddy had to hold her arm and take her down and then she was slow. (There are forty two steps.)

Weddy is a very nice person and very friendly, and I shall be very sad when she dies.

Schoolgirl (aged 10)

297   The Cut

There was a scrambling thud and shriek, which changed to howls.

'Mummy!' Tabitha bellowed. 'I fell.'

Sue stopped the car and looked back. The middle drawer of the bureau was partly open, and Tabitha was struggling to her feet from the floor beside it.

'My leg!' she wailed. 'It hurts!'

She looked down and shrieked again, this time in terror.

'It's bleeding! Mummy! Mummy!'

It was indeed bleeding—pouring, in fact, down Tabitha's leg into a spreading pool on the car floor.

Tabitha's yells ceased from sheer paralysis of fright.

Sue never remembered getting over into the back of the station wagon, but by the time she reached Tabitha her professional mind had taken firm charge of her emotions.

A vein had been cut, she saw—not an artery, for the blood poured steadily in the split seconds before her hands closed around Tabitha's leg, below the jagged wound which was on the inner side, just under the knee.

The flow became a trickle, a slight ooze—stopped.

But she couldn't kneel here indefinitely, holding it back. She must contrive some kind of tourniquet and reassure the blue faced Tabs who was looking at her mother in desperate appeal.

'Darling,' said Sue's professional voice, 'don't be frightened. I'll fix it. Does it hurt much now?'

'N-no. It-it's the blood, Mummy.'

'But blood isn't anything, my sweet. I've told you that. And anyway it's stopped. Can you help me a little by doing what I tell you?'

'I'll try?' Tabs quavered.

'Good! Then sit down against the side of the car. That's a little hard when I'm holding your leg, but you can do it. That's right. Now take hold of your leg, just the way I'm doing—hard—with both hands.'

Tabs leaned against the car and gripped with both pudgy hands, just above Sue's.

'That's my girl! Squeeze! Squeeze harder! I'm going to find something to tie around so we won't have to hold it. Let's see how you're doing.'

Sue let go, and there was an instant welling of blood. Tabitha whimpered.

'Hold tighter,' Sue ordered. 'Terribly tight.'

The flow ceased and Tabitha looked up proudly, a little more colour in her face.

'Splendid,' said Sue. 'Even Cal couldn't do better. Hold it just like that, and if it starts to bleed don't let go! Grab harder!'

'All right, Mummy.'

Sue was thinking rapidly. There was no use in trying to tear a piece of her dress or Tabitha's. The material was new and tough. She thought briefly of rubber covered light or horn wires in the car. No, she'd be for ever getting them out. And she had brought no handkerchief. What was worse, her bag had no strap on it long enough to go round.

She glanced out of the car window and brightened.

'I'll be right back,' she told Tabs, and jumping out of the car, leaped across the ditch and up the low embankment to the field beyond. She snatched a large handful of long grass, twisted it, and tried it on her own ankle. A few of the stems broke, but the general mass held firmly. Now for a stick!

She hurried back to the fallen limb and broke off a sizable green twig.

'Here we are,' she said to Tabitha. 'Hold on just a second more.'

She tied the twist of grass in place, thrust the stick through the knot and turned it.

'That hurts, Mummy,' Tabs protested.

'I know, dear, but we can't help it. It's just till we get home. You hold the stick so it won't turn back.'

She lifted Tabs over into the front seat.

'Keep your leg straight out, darling. I'll get home as fast as I can, and we'll call Daddy.'

The car tilted on to the highway, and Sue stepped on the gas, one eye on Tabitha's leg. There would have to be stitches—and quite a disinfecting job, for a flap of skin was turned in. Furthermore she didn't know how long Tabitha would be able to keep the grass tourniquet tight. Poor baby! She was crying quietly, now, and Sue made no attempt to stop her. The child had had a shock and this was a good way of getting it out of her system.

From Sue Barton, Neighbourhood Nurse *by Helen Dore Boylston*

Appendix 1: Hymns

The type of hymn which a school uses in its assembly depends very much on a combination of considerations. These might include the attitude of the staff to assemblies, the skill of the teachers with regard to playing accompaniments, the type and quantity of hymn books available, the quality of the children's own musical groups.

In my opinion what the children sing and play is of very great importance to the success of the assembly as a whole. In consequence when choosing the hymns which follow I have been guided by a number of features. These might be summarised as follows:

1 Each hymn chosen has a relevance to one, or in most cases, more of the themes chosen.
2 Particular attention has been paid to the words of each hymn chosen so that, like the material in the rest of the book, they might provoke thought and discussion.
3 Most of the tunes chosen have got a strong rhythmic quality but none are difficult with regard to piano accompaniment.
4 I have tried to include a good number of hymns which lend themselves to 'children only' accompaniment. By this I mean the usual combination of recorders, chime bars, percussion, etc.
5 All the hymns chosen are ones which I have heard children singing with enjoyment.

With regard to practical considerations, and ease of reference, two other points must be mentioned. Although some of the hymns and songs which follow can be found fairly easily in a number of books, the sources which I suggest are, in my opinion, valuable books to have in school.

Secondly, to link each hymn with a specific theme would be a complex task, and increase the difficulties of reference in using the book. To alleviate this problem I have set out hymn suggestions under five headings. When a theme and suitable extracts to illustrate it have been chosen these headings should be consulted and it should be found that one or more is relevant to the theme. Hymns may then be chosen from under the relevant headings. The five headings are:

1 **Personal Questions**
2 **Social Concerns**
3 **The Important Issues in Life**
4 **Festivals and Faith**
5 **World Around Us**

Thus each hymn will appear under one of these titles, and it will be followed by one or more of these symbols:

A to J—which will indicate the book in which it can be found.
X—which will indicate that this particular hymn is especially suitable for children's instrumental accompaniment.
Y—which will indicate that this is a hymn most suited for the younger members of the seven to eleven age range.

The hymn books recommended are:

A   *Sing Life, Sing Love* Holmes McDougall
B   *In Every Corner Sing* Nelson
C   *Hymns for Today* High Fye Music Ltd.
D   *Come to Bethlehem* Vanguard Music Ltd.
E   *So Much to Sing* Vanguard Music Ltd.
F   *Hello World* Galliard
G   *New Horizons* Galliard
H   *With Cheerful Voice* A. C. Black
I   *New Orbit* Galliard
J   *Morning has Broken* Schofield and Sims

1 **Personal Questions** suggested Hymns:

'Word of Love' A
'When I Needed a Neighbour' A, X
'Thank You' A, X
'Can It Be True?' B
'Go It Alone' B
'I Must Walk This Lonesome Valley' B
'Everyone Has a Job to Do' F, X, Y
'So Here Hath Been Dawning' H
'Every Day Brings Us New Chances' I, X

'Lord I Love to Stamp' I
'I'm Very Glad of God' J, X, Y

2 Social Concerns suggested Hymns:

'There but for Fortune' A
'If I Had a Hammer' B
'Shelter the Weak' C
'Nativity' E
'Hold Out a Hand' E
'The Hungry Man' E, X
'Shalom Chaverim' H, X
'Strangest Dream' H, X
'One Man's Hands' H, X
'It is Good to Give a Meal' I
'The Ink is Black' I

3 The Important Issues in Life suggested Hymns:

'The Family of Man' A, X
'We Shall Overcome' A, X
'Only a Fool' A
'We Ask That We Live' B
'Tomorrow Is a Highway' B
'Come Workers for the Lord' B, X
'Here's Joy!' E, X
'Shelter Makes the Home and Family' F, X, Y
'Dial 999 Emergency' G, Y
'Sad Faces, Happy Faces' G, Y
'Where, Oh Where's My Silver Piece?' G, Y
'Lord of all Hopefulness' H
'Joy is Meant for Giving' IX
'A Little Tiny Bird' J, Y
'Give Me Joy in My Heart' J, X
'God Whose Name is Love' J, X/Y

4 Festivals and Faith suggested Hymns:

'Sing Life, Sing Love, Sing Jesus' A
'Lord of the Dance' A, X
'Kum Bah Yah' A, X
'Gentle Christ' A, X

'Every Star Shall Sing a Carol' B
'Star in the East' D, X
'Christmas Prayer' D
'Asleep to the World' D
'Harvest Time' E
'Mary Set Out on a Winter's Night' F, X, Y
'Mary Had a Baby' G, X, Y
'At Work beside his Father's Bench' H
'Standing in the rain' I
'The Good Things of the Earth' J

5 The World Around Us suggested Hymns:

'The Summer Days Are Come Again' B, X
'God Whose Farm Is All Creation' B
'God of Concrete, God of Steel' B, X
'Gifts' C
'Time' C
'A Song of Joy' E
'The "Do It Yourself" Thank You' E, X
'Lights Go Up in the City' F, X, Y
'The Steelworks' F, X, Y
'There Are Houses and Houses' G, X, Y
'O Listen to the Sounds of the World' G, Y
'Sing We of the Modern City' I
'Think of a World without Any Flowers' I
'Come Let Us Remember the Joys of the Town' I, X
'To God Who Makes All Lovely Things' J, X, Y
'I Love the Sun' J, Y
'Daisies Are Our Silver' J, X, Y

Appendix 2: Records

When considering the use of records in assemblies two reservations immediately suggest themselves: a poor assembly is not likely to be rectified by an inspired choice of recorded material; yet a good assembly can lose much of its effect if over familiar, or unsuitable records are played.

As most schools seem to consider the use of records an essential assembly requirement, it is important to assess their suitability, originality and purpose when choosing what to use. Having 'introductory music' to which the children enter the hall should not for instance mean the repetitive employment of over familiar, often scratched, records. The variety of introductory music should be as rich as the variety of themes. If the theme of the assembly is a 'joyous' one, then obviously *Carnival of the Animals* would provide a more satisfactory introductory selection than *Danse Macabre*.

To let the children sing as they enter the hall is often a worthwhile and enjoyable experience. What better stimulus in this context then, than one of the B.B.C. collections such as *Songs for Assembly*.

It may well also be that when the 'words' of an assembly are finished a particularly evocative choice of music will emphasize and enhance them. After all, a musician as influential as Mahler suggested that 'music begins where words leave off'.

Of course the use of words on record is an important assembly consideration too. These might be spoken or sung. Similarly, another assembly might have its effectiveness enhanced by the use of recorded sound effects.

The record list which follows aims to provide material to cover all these features. Where the record has been designated 'background/mood/effect' material, the choice of extract and suitability to theme will obviously be decided upon by the presenter or presenters.

The effects records are for reference.

I have given fuller details of those records which contain 'selections'. This will provide information to those who may consider buying them. Also, some of these records contain interesting words to listen to, or to sing along with.

1 Records for General Background/Mood/Effect

Tchaikovsky *Romeo and Juliet*   WING WL 1012
(Overture & Fantasia)
Schubert *Symphony No. 8 in B Minor (Unfinished)*

Tchaikovsky *Swan Lake*   FIDELIO TLS 6021
Bizet *Carmen*

Delibes *Copellia and Sylvia Ballet Suites*   WING WL 1135
Gounod *Faust Ballet Music*

Mozart *Eine Kleine Nachtmusik*   COLUMBIA C 70461
Haydn *Kindersinfonie*

Wagner *The Flying Dutchman*   HELIODOR 89652
(particularly Overture)

Scott Joplin *Prodigal Son*   CBS 73363

Beethoven *Egmont, Coriolan, Fidelio, Prometheus* WING WL 1147
and Leonore Overtures

Saint-Saens *Carnival of Animals*   RCA CAMDEN CDS 1034
Grieg *Peer Gynt*

Borodin *Polovtsian Dances*   ARC FDY 2045
Mussorgsky *Night on a Bare Mountain*

Holst *The Planets*   H.M.V. ASD 2301

Favourite Concert Melodies   MARBLE ARCH MAL 778
Bach *Air*, Mozart *Turkish March*, Schubert *Rosamunde*, Wagner *Tannhauser*, Tchaikovsky *Waltz of the Flowers*, Liszt *Liebestraum*, Wagner *Lohengrin* Bridal Chorus, Schumann *Traumerei*

The World of Your Hundred Best Tunes—Top Ten DECCA SPA 112
Sibelius *Finlandia*, Mascagni *Cavalleria Rusticana*, Beethoven *Pastoral* First Movt. and *Moonlight Sonata*, Verdi *Nabucco* Slave Chorus

244

Ten Top Classics   CONTOUR 6870526
Mozart Allegro from *40th Sym.*, Bach *Badinerie*, Dvorak
Serenade in D Minor, Beethoven 9th Sym. Final Chorus,
Khatchaturian *Sabre Dance*, Rachmaninov *Prelude*, Saint-Saens
Danse Macabre

2 Effects

B.B.C. Sound Effects No. 1   RED 47M

Some British Accents and Dialects   B.B.C. RESR 28M

3 Spoken Message

God's Brainwave   ACE OF CLUBS ACL 324
Bernard Miles on 'ten to eight'

The Hopwood Family   B.B.C. RESR 9

4 Sung Message

Songs for Assembly   B.B.C. RESR 15
'Sing Levy Dew', 'If I had a Hammer', 'Every Star Shall Sing a
Carol', 'The Crow and the Cradle', 'Dust and Ashes', 'Standing
in the Rain', 'Judas and Mary', 'Where I'm Bound', 'Sinner
Man', 'Bitter Was the Night', 'Sympathy', 'Let Loose', 'Dives
and Lazarus', 'If You Want to Go to Freedom', 'Streets of
London'

Songs Are for Singing   B.B.C. RESR 18
'Swing Low', 'Little David Play Your Harp', 'Trotting Through
Jerusalem', 'Easter Eggs', 'Glad That I Live Am I', 'Golden
Sheaves', 'Holly and the Ivy', 'Patapan', 'Mary's Child',
'Cowboy Carol', 'Lord's Prayer'

New Life   B.B.C. RESR 295
'Spirit', 'Go Peacefully', 'New Life', 'Shape of Things to Come',
'Best Way of All', 'You Need My Lord', 'Everybody Sing',
'Maureen and Billy', 'Looking Good', 'I Am Much More', 'Long
Lost Cause', 'Kum Bah yah'

Get Together   B.B.C. RED 147 S
'The Building Song', 'What Is the Meaning of Life', 'I Listen, and
I Listen', 'Spirit of God', 'Love Came a Tricklin' Down',

'Watching and Waiting', 'All My Trials', 'Morning Has
Broken', 'See Him Lying on a Bed of Straw', 'There's a Man For
All People', 'Wonderful World', 'Get Together'

Get on Board   COLUMBIA 335X 1370
A marvellous selection of negro spirituals sung with
tremendous verve and rhythm by the Golden Gate Quartet

Fourpence a Day   GALLIARD GAL 4015
(Folk song selection)

And Now It Is So Early   GALLIARD GAL 4017
Songs of Sydney Carter

Joseph and the Amazing Technicolour   DECCA SKL 4973
Dream Coat

Godspell   BELLS 203

Cabaret   PROBE SPB 1052
Judicious selection needed here but some fascinating material
available: 'If You Could See Her Through My Eyes', 'Money'

Storytime   E.M.I. CLP 1909
Interesting story collection which includes 'The Pied Piper', and
is backed by a virile Dixieland band which children enjoy

Black and Blue; Saint Louis Blues   PHILIPS 429 650 BE
Some evocative blues by the Louis Armstrong All Stars, with
the words of 'Black and Blue' being particularly thought-
provoking.

Acknowledgements

Acknowledgements and thanks are due to:
The many children whose contributions are contained in this book. Headmasters of the
following schools who have given permission for work by their children to be
included: Saint Clements Junior School, Goffs School, Cheshunt School, Saint Mary's
High School, all of Cheshunt. Particular help was given by Miss Elspeth Jamieson, Head
of Religious Education at Saint Mary's School, and other material was also contributed
by children of Dewhurst Saint Mary School, Cheshunt. Mr Geraint Lloyd-Evans,
Hertfordshire County English Adviser, for permission to use material written by other
children throughout the county. Jack Edwards for his comments on the history of
Dewhurst School, taken from his book *Cheshunt in Hertfordshire*. The Reverend R. O.
Osborne for a passage from one of his church newsletters. The Editor of *See Round*, the
Saint Albans diocesan news sheet, for permission to use material from this magazine.

The author and publishers also wish to thank the following, who have given permission for the use of copyright material:

Ernest Benn Limited for 'The Shooting of Dan McGrew' from *Poems* and 'The Ordinary Man' from *Songs of a Sun Lover* by Robert Service. Blandford Press Limited for the poem 'Working for People' by J Morrison from *Poems for the School Assembly and other occasions*. Edited by D M Prescott. The Bodley Head for 'The Cut' from *Sue Barton, Neighbourhood Nurse* by Helen Dore Boylston. Cambridge University Press for extract from *New English Bible*, second edition © 1970 by permission of Oxford and Cambridge University Presses. Jonathan Cape Limited for extracts from *Miss Carter Wore Pink* by Helen Bradley and 'Taking the Hands' from *Silence in the Snowy Fields* by Robert Bly. Jonathan Cape Limited on behalf of Mrs H M Davies for 'Leisure' and 'School's Out' from *The Complete Poems* of W H Davies. Jonathan Cape Limited on behalf of the Executors of the Bernard Pares Estate, for 'Crow and Fox' from *Krylov's Fables* translated by Bernard Pares. William Collins Sons & Company Limited for extract from *Mister God, This Is Anna* by Fynn. Jeni Couzyn for the poem 'My Father's Hands'. Darton Longman & Todd Limited for extracts from *Jerusalem Bible* published and © 1966, 1967, 1968 by Darton Longman & Todd Limited and Doubleday & Company Inc and is used by permission of the publishers. J M Dent & Sons Limited for the poems 'Fox' from *Poems 1935–48* by Clifford Dyment and 'The People Upstairs' from *Versus* by Ogden Nash. Andre Deutsch Limited Publishers for the poems 'I Share my Bedroom with my Brother' and 'Boy' from *Mind Your Own Business* by Michael Rosen. Ronald Dingwall for 'Freedom' by Kaye Chudley from *Assembly Workshop* edited by Ronald Dingwall. Eyre & Spottiswoode (Publishers) Limited for the poem 'Growing Pains' by Vernon Scannell from *Epithets of War 1965–69*. Faber & Faber Limited for extracts 'Hedgehog' from *New Weather* by Paul Muldoon, 'Funeral Blues' from *Collected Shorter Poems 1927–57* by W H Auden, 'Days' from *Whitsun Weddings* by Philip Larkin and 'A Peaceful Solution' from *The Iron Man* by Ted Hughes. Gill & Macmillan Limited for 'Lord I Have Time' and 'Housing' from *Prayers of Life* by Michel Quoist. Victor Gollancz Limited for extract from *Carrie's War* by Nina Bawden. Granada Publishing Limited for extract 'An Old Lady I Know' from *The Excitement of Writing* edited by A B Clegg. Published by Chatto & Windus Educational Limited. Reverend F Pratt Green for his poem 'The Victim died of Stab Wounds'. The Guardian Newspapers Limited for extracts 'Medal for bomb hero' 17-12-74 and 'Hero' 26-11-74. Harcourt Brace Jovanovich Inc for 'What Kind of Liar are You?' from *The People Yes* by Carl Sandburg. George G Harrap & Company Limited for 'The Well Off Kid' by Bill Naughton from *The Goalkeeper's Revenge*. William Heinemann Limited for 'The New Boy' from *The Truants* by John Walsh. Help the Aged International Appeal organised by Voluntary & Christian Service for extract from their poster. Hertfordshire Countryside for extract 'Mad Lucas' by Elissa Milsome. Norman Hidden for the poems 'I wish I were' by D Chisnall and 'A Dormitory Suburb' by Jenny Scott from *Say It Aloud* Edited by Norman Hidden. David Higham Associates Limited for the poems 'Song of the Battery Hen' by Edwin Brock from *Penguin Modern Poets*, published by Penguin, 'Timothy Winters' from *Union Street* by Charles Causley, published by Hart Davis; 'My Mother saw a dancing Bear' from *Figgin Hobbin* by Charles Causley and 'Schoolmistress' from *Dorset Village* by Clive Sansom, published by Methuen. Holmes McDougall Limited for the song 'Dazzling New and Super You' by Roy Lawrence from *Sing Life, Sing Love*. Hope Leresche & Steel for 'Goodbat Nightman' by Roger McGough. Copyright © Roger McGough from *Penguin Modern Poets 10*. Hutchinson Publishing Group Limited for 'Watching a Bird' by Michael from *Young Writers Young Readers* Edited by Boris Ford. Michael Joseph Limited for extract from *A Kestrel For a Knave* by Barry Hines. Katherine B Kavanagh for 'Tinker's Wife' from *Collected Poems* by Patrick Kavanagh. James Kirkup for his poems 'Cena' and 'The Lonely Scarecrow'. Lindsay Levy for her poem 'Edinburgh Rain and Love Poem'. The London Magazine for 'Arithmetic' by Gavin Ewart. Lutterworth Press for extract from *The House of Sixty Fathers* by Meindert Dejong. Ian Macdonald for 'Georgetown Children' from *Outposts*.

247

Macmillan Publishing Company Inc, New York for the poems 'Something told the Wildgeese' from *Poems* by Rachel Field. Copyright 1934 by Macmillan Publishing Company Inc, renewed 1967 by Arthur S Pederson and 'An Indian Summer Day on the Prairie' from *Collected Poems* by Vachel Lindsay. Copyright 1914 by Macmillan Publishing Company Inc., renewed 1942 by Elizabeth C Lindsay. Wes Magee for the story *Trapped*. McGraw-Hill Ryerson Limited for 'The Man Who Finds His Son Has Become a Thief' from *The Colour of The Times/Ten Elephants on Yonge Street* by Raymond Souster, reprinted by permission of the publisher. John Murray (Publishers) Limited for 'Harvest Hymn' by John Betjeman from *Collected Poems*. National Council of The Churches of Christ for extract from the Revised Standard Version of the Bible, copyrighted 1946, 1952, © 1971, 1973 and used by permission. Robert Nye for the poem 'The Long Ago Boy'. Oxford University Press for extract 'The Love Affair' by Vian Smith from *Miscellany Six* and the poem 'Posting Letters' from *Posting Letters* by Gregory Harrison. Penguin Books Limited for 'The Companion' from *Yevtushenko: Selected Poems*, translated by Robin Milner-Gulland and Peter Levi from *Penguin Modern European Poets*, 1962. Lawrence Pollinger Limited and the Estate of the late Mrs Frieda Lawrence for 'New Houses, New Clothes' from *The Complete Poems* of D H Lawrence and an extract from 'Adolf' from *Phoenix* by D H Lawrence, published by William Heinemann Limited. Douglas Rae Management Limited and Evan Jones for 'Lament of the Banana Man' from *Caribbean Voices* 1966, published by Evans Bros (Books) Limited. Celia Randall for her poem 'Boy into a Heron'. The Royal Institute for the Deaf for extract from 'Educating Deaf Children' from R.N.I.D., 105 Gower Street, London WC1E 6AH pamphlet. Royal National Life-Boat Institution for extract from R.N.L.I. poster. The Saint Andrew Press for 'Echo Valley' by John D Searle from *Look and Listen through the Year*. G T Sassoon for the poem 'Middle Ages' by Siegfried Sassoon. Ian Crichton Smith for his poem 'Rythm' from *Law and the Grace*. The Society of Authors on behalf of the Literary Trustees of Walter de la Mare for 'Done For' by Walter de la Mare. Stainer & Bell Limited for 'One more Step' by Sydney Carter from *Green Print for Song*. Teachers World for use of Carol; The Sea Changes Everything; Barren Creek's Christmas Gifts; The Chess Match, The Bus; Dear Editors; and New Boy from Teachers World Edited by R Deadman, published by Evans Bros. Limited. The Daily Telegraph for extract 'Police Leave Cancelled' 29-4-75, 'Centenary Exhibition of Marconi' 25-4-74, 'Right to Serve' 23-5-74, 'A Child's View of the War' 26-4-74 and 'Thousands will Die' 27-4-75. Reverend E M Turner for extract from his 'Little guide to visitors to Eyam Church'. Henry Z Walck Inc. Publishers for 'Sing a Song of People' from *The Life I Live* by Lois Lenski. Copyright 1965 by Lois Lenski. Reprinted by permission. A P Watt & Son for extract from *The Jungle Book* by Rudyard Kipling. Eric W Williams for extract from the Introduction to *The Wooden Horse* (published by Collins) in which the author, Eric Williams, describes his escape from a German prison camp 1943.

The author and publishers wish to acknowledge the following photograph sources:

Ron Chapman, Colorsport, Imperial War Museum, Sheelah Latham, London Express Pictures and the Meteorological Office.

The publishers have made every effort to trace the copyright holders, of written and illustrative material, but if they have inadvertently overlooked any, they will be pleased to make the necessary arrangement at the first opportunity.

Index of Titles and Authors

Poetry

Prose

255